OPPOSITIONAL DEFIANT

DISORDER

The Best Behaviour Management Strategies for Children with Cases of ODD that Could Lead to Psychopathy - Stop Temper Tantrums Before They Start!

DAVID LAWSON PhD

TABLE OF CONTENTS

INTRODUCTION

Oppositional defiant disorder is a relatively new addition to the DSM, however, this does not mean it is something that has just happened. It is estimated that around 10% of children worldwide will develop ODD, with many of them carrying the associated manifestations well into adulthood.

A child who suffers from this disruptive behavior disorder can be identified by analyzing his/her daily existence. He/she will be the child to constantly defy figures of authority, with frequent temper tantrums or outbursts of anger. Easily irritated and often frustrated, he/she will delight in arguments and power struggles.

In this book, we have presented a wealth of useful information on ODD. You will be able to read about the manifestations of this behavioral disorder so that you can decide whether your child is at risk. You will discover that ODD often co-exists with other conditions, such as ADHD, mood and anxiety disorders. More importantly, left unaddressed, it can lead to conduct disorders and drug abuse.

Of course, you have every right to wonder what may have caused your child to become oppositional and defiant. In the second chapter, we present theories on why ODD appears, as well as potential causes, such as family history, negative reinforcement from parents and neurobiological impairments. You can read all about risk factors and the age at which the condition can be diagnosed.

Find out about the evaluation used for the diagnosis of ODD and the assessment tools one might use to confirm it. Read about bad parenting and how it can influence the appearance of behavioral issues. For instance, did you know that children thrive from negative attention, so they might engage in destructive behavior just to get you to see them?

It often happens that ODD co-exists with other conditions, such as anxiety, depression or learning disabilities. Discover the connection between behavioral and mental health issues, as well as how to help a child who suffers from such issues. Check out the dangers of untreated ODD – the behavior is only bound to get worse, and there is a considerable risk of drug abuse, conduct disorder, and violence.

We want to strongly emphasize that early intervention will see the best results for someone who suffers from ODD. The sooner therapy is started, the better chance your child has of turning into a healthy, functional adult. You cannot simply ignore the issue in the hope that it will go away. This is a behavioral issue and it must be addressed – a good parent will attack the root cause, seeking out the most effective solutions against the problematic behavior.

We will also talk about the differences between children and teenagers who suffer from ODD. You need to be aware of these, as the age of the child will dictate not only your approach but also the intervention solutions. For instance, while a child might benefit from therapy and quality time with his/her parents, for teenagers, medication and therapy might offer better results.

Nowadays, a lot of research is dedicated to discovering what happens in the brain of children and teenagers diagnosed with behavioral issues. It has been confirmed that such children/teenagers may have a neurotransmitter imbalance, which can lead to problematic behavior. Read about brain development and find out why your child's "flight-or-fight" response may be permanently activated.

Once you understand how your child's brain works, you will also be able to understand why they do certain things. Such children do not process punishment in the typical way, they have a reduced interest in rewards and often cannot control their emotions. So, you see, aside from therapy, you need to work to understand your child. And we are here to help you, with each chapter containing plenty of useful information.

When it comes to behavioral issues, people tend to consider all children with ODD the same. While they might share common characteristics, it is useful to mention that each child has a unique symptom profile. As a parent, you are the closest observer and you can identify your child's patterns of behavior, sharing your conclusions with the therapist. You just need to monitor your child and look for red flags, behavior-wise.

As this book is dedicated to parents, we want to help you understand how to deal with an oppositional defiant child effectively. We have included advice on how to avoid power struggles and model the desired behavior for the child. We have come up with solutions on how to discipline a child who refuses to listen and how to create healthy boundaries.

The relationship between a parent and a child can be difficult at times, especially when ODD is an issue. We hope to help you overcome obstacles and learn how to act when your child is unable to voice his/her concerns. There is also a chapter on how to manage at school and we always make the recommendation that parents should collaborate with teachers, as this is in the best interest of the child.

A chapter has been dedicated to addressing spoiled behavior, as this can often make manifestations of ODD worse. We have added information on how to properly manage extreme behavior, reducing the risk of aggression and violence. Last, but not least, we have included useful tips on how to create a healthy long-term relationship with your child, and a plan highlighting all the steps to be followed.

In the final part of the book, we have included four case studies. Each case study is worth paying attention to, as it presents the story of a child or teenager who has managed to come out the other side of ODD, and all thanks to having a plan. Therapy seems to work best for children and teenagers, and it is essential to remember that sometimes ODD can be present in adults as well.

We hope you will enjoy the book and recommend it to other parents who are trying to deal with an oppositional and defiant child. Always remember that a child needs to feel loved above all else. You are his/her safe space and you can help him/her overcome ODD, and grow into a healthy and well-adjusted adult.

CHAPTER 1 - WHAT IS OPPOSITIONAL DEFIANT DISORDER (ODD)?

O ppositional defiant disorder can be defined as a behavioral problem, which is commonly diagnosed in young children. Because any child can exhibit this kind of behavior, it falls to parents to recognize an ongoing negative pattern that may affect school performance, social activities, family relationships and so on.

A child or teenager who suffers from oppositional defiant disorder will be difficult and challenging, exhibiting frequent bouts of irritability, defiance or anger. He/she will choose to argue with family, peers or authority figures, often going as far as being vengeful or vindictive.

Upon recognizing such behavior, parents must take the child or teenager to a specialist. Once an accurate diagnosis has been made, behavioral therapy will most likely follow, not only for the ODD but also for any associated mental health issues, such as ADHD.

As you will read in the coming chapters, the main idea behind this therapy is to help the child/teenager develop skills for positive interactions, as well as implementing strategies for overcoming the problematic behavior. Medication should remain the last resort, being used only in the most severe cases.

Of course, it can be difficult to determine whether a child/teenager suffers from oppositional defiant disorder or if he/she is just going through a normal developmental stage. Children who are emotional or strong-willed often cause others to believe they are suffering from ODD.

Defiant child? He/she might suffer from oppositional defiant disorder!

All children, teenagers included, can exhibit signs of opposition. These negative patterns are sometimes reinforced by family dynamics, but there is still a long way to go until one can say that an actual problem exists. Parents, with the help of specialists, should recognize the difference between the two types of behavior.

One thing to remember that oppositional behavior is normal up to a certain point, being suggestive of healthy development. However, when it comes to ODD, one must learn to look for red flags, which can be present as early as the preschool years. The behavior, if not corrected, can affect the overall quality of life, preventing one from becoming a healthy and functional adult.

How does this condition manifest? What are the signs?

Upon suffering from oppositional defiant disorder, one will present both emotional and behavioral manifestations. Children and teenagers with ODD are often angry and easily irritable. They lose their temper effortlessly, are described as "touchy" by parents or peers, and they find the slightest reason to become annoyed with other people. Resentful, they will almost always seek to blame others for the things that happen to them.

Defiant behavior does not appear on its own, often being accompanied by a multitude of arguments. One will take pleasure in arguing with authority figures, parents and even peers. He/she might refuse to commit to rules or will actively defy the requests of adults. When mistakes are made, sufferers of ODD will seek to blame others.

For the condition to be considered ODD and not just a passing stage in normal development, the behavior must be present at least several times over six months. This can include spiteful or vindictive behavior, in different ranges of severity.

In mild cases, the behavior will be present in a single setting, most commonly at home, but it can also be seen at school or when interacting with peers. In moderate to severe cases, the behavior will occur in more than one setting, often overlapping with other negative behaviors. Initially, the signs are noticeable only in the home environment, being visible in other settings at a later stage.

One should not expect the child to acknowledge his/her behavior as a problem

Children/teenagers who suffer from ODD will rarely acknowledge that their behavior is not normal. They will often seek to blame others, making unreasonable demands or being defiant, uncooperative, etc. The negative behavior becomes more obvious when one is upset, sad, tired or hungry, disrupting the relationships with other people, especially family.

In smaller children, the behavior often appears in the form of frequent temper tantrums. They may also question rules, speaking impolitely to their parents or other authority figures. Vindictiveness can be issue, with most children with ODD seeking revenge.

Oppositional-defiant disorder appears either as a result of a developmental problem, or it can be a learned behavior. Parents might have difficulties dealing with such a child, often displaying extreme behavior themselves. They will either permit the child/teenager to behave in any way he/she wants, or they will become coercive. Such behaviors will not change the one of the child; on the contrary, they will only aggravate the matter.

The parents' behavior concerning ODD can lead to more negative interactions and can reinforce the child's pattern of behavior until it becomes a regular habit. The disorder can play a significant role in family relationships, with both the child and the parents experiencing frustration.

Parents have to deal with a child or a teenager who fails to listen to them, always arguing and suffering from tantrums or outbursts. These tend to accumulate over time, affecting the relationship between the parents and the child. This is especially seen in children/teenagers who suffer from other conditions, such as attention deficit disorder, depression, anxiety or learning disabilities.

Some children behave in such a manner to annoy or upset the people around them, especially parents or other authority figures. In teenagers, using swear words or obscene language might be preferred. Moodiness, visible signs of frustration and reduced self-esteem might accompany the behavior of the child/teenager suffering from ODD. There is also a potential risk of alcohol or drug abuse.

It is estimated that 16% of children worldwide suffer from oppositional defiant disorder. In some, especially toddlers or teens, the diagnosis can difficult to be make; this is because ODD and the typical independence-seeking behavior share common characteristics.

There is also a difference between boys and girls who suffer from ODD. Males often exhibit tendencies towards physical aggression, with sudden outbursts of anger and frustration. Girls, on the other hand, are uncooperative, preferring to withhold the truth.

Children can outgrow the condition on their own, but this does not happen often. Early intervention, with adequate treatment plans, will correct the oppositional behavior and prevent the progression towards a conduct disorder, or more severe mental health issues.

Identifying what your child suffers from – ODD, conduct disorder, ADHD, antisocial personality

As a parent, it is only normal to want the best for your child. Upon noticing that something is wrong, you might also experience confusion about what is happening. Many behavioral issues share common manifestations, so getting confused is something that happens quite often.

Oppositional defiant disorder is defined, as mentioned, by emotional and behavioral symptoms – the child is angry and irritable, he/she becomes defiant in the face of rules and prefers arguing with parents and authority figures. Children might also be spiteful or vindictive, with the overall changes taking place over six months or more.

The conduct disorder often evolves from ODD, being more commonly diagnosed during adolescence. It is characterized by behaviors that involve breaking the rules and is considered a precursor to an antisocial personality. The child or adolescent can become violent, experiencing adjustment problems.

Attention deficit hyperactivity disorder, often abbreviated as ADHD, is a neurodevelopmental disorder. Children who suffer from ADHD have high levels of energy, they find it difficult to stay in one place or concentrate on a specific task. The condition can affect school performance, and can transfer well into adulthood.

Antisocial personality disorder is a mental health problem in which the person has a clear disregard for the rights of other people. He/she might go as far as to violate these rights. People who suffer from this condition will often have problems with the law, being manipulative and deceitful.

CHAPTER 2 – WHY DOES YOUR CHILD HAVE OPPOSITIONAL DEFIANT DISORDER?

D espite extensive research, there is no confirmed cause of oppositional defiant disorder. A combination of factors has been proposed, including genetic, environmental and neurobiological. Parents have every right to wonder why their child suffers from ODD, but they should pay attention to the family environment and other factors contributing to the problem.

Theories – is ODD a developmental issue or a learned behavior?

There are two main theories related to the occurrence of oppositional defiant disorder.

The first is known as the developmental theory and it suggests that the first signs of ODD are visible from toddlerhood. These are the children who will have difficulty becoming independent, being excessively attached to their parents or other caregivers. In this case, ODD is considered a developmental issue, which will be reflected in later years.

The learning theory, on the other hand, suggests that ODD is an acquired behavior. The child will develop opposition and defiance as a result of negative reinforcement, coming from parents and/or other authority figures. It is often said that attention, whether positive or negative, is still attention and the child wants it. In ODD, the child gets both attention and reaction, leading them to continue with the oppositional and defiant behavior.

Genetic factors

Children who have a genetic predisposition towards impulsive behavior might develop ODD as well. It has been confirmed that there are neurobiological differences between children with ODD and those who do not suffer from this condition. These are the children with a difficult temperament, who have trouble controlling impulses or demand rewards for everything.

Environmental

The family environment is one of the main factors incriminated in the appearance of this disorder. Children who are abused or neglected present a higher risk of developing ODD, as do those who are disciplined through harsh methods. Lack of supervision and inconsistent parenting practices may add to the problem.

Often, manifestations of ODD are strengthened through negative attention from peers, family members or authority figures. This can be a vicious cycle, with the child eliciting the behavior and the adults reinforcing it through negative interactions. Inconsistent discipline from additional authority figures, such as teachers, can aggravate the condition.

The more often the negative interactions are repeated, the more severe the manifestations of ODD will become. Children who had difficulties regulating their emotions at a young age will likely continue on the same path later; they will find it hard to regulate behavior, especially when it comes to anger, frustration, and disappointment. Many adolescents are thus diagnosed with ODD.

Parents are hugely responsible for the behavior of their children. Negative interactions will always cause the child to behave in any way other than the one accepted. Conflicts between parents and children make oppositional defiant disorder more noticeable, as do insecure attachments.

Neurobiological

Children with minor brain defects or those who have suffered a traumatic brain injury can develop ODD. Manifestations of this disorder have been associated with abnormal functioning of brain neurotransmitters. These are responsible for healthy communication between different brain regions; when they fail to work, they might affect areas controlling behavior, reasoning, and impulse.

Neurotransmitters play an important role in the neural systems which regulate behavioral responses to negative and positive emotions. Some children seem to have an overactive behavioral activation system, responding easily to negative reinforcement. On the other hand, their behavioral inhibition system is underactive, which means they will have difficulties regulating their emotions.

Risk factors

A child who has difficulties regulating his/her emotions and behavior is prone to suffering from oppositional defiant disorder. Such children tend to react excessively to seemingly neutral situations, or they may have a hard time tolerating their frustrations.

Children who grow up in dysfunctional families, in which there is constant fighting, alcohol or drug abuse, may also suffer from ODD. The same goes for the children whose parents suffer from various mental health issues, such as depression, anxiety or borderline personality disorder. These children are more vulnerable in the face of behavioral issues. It seems that children who come from families with a low socioeconomic status present a higher risk of ODD.

Other factors

Gender seems to be a risk factor. Oppositional defiant disorder is more common in boys during childhood, and the condition is more often diagnosed in girls after puberty. Additional health issues, such as learning disorders, mood or anxiety disorders, might also increase the risk of ODD.

Oppositional defiant disorder is sometimes diagnosed in children or adolescents who have experienced major life stresses, such as parents getting divorced, death in the family or financial hardship. Physical trauma can lead to ODD as well.

Problems during pregnancy or birth can prepare the terrain for ODD. Malnourished children, especially those who suffer from protein deficiency, such as those who have been diagnosed with lead poisoning, are at risk of this condition. The same goes for those whose mothers consumed alcohol or drugs during pregnancy.

In some children or adolescents, cognitive impairment has been associated with oppositional defiant disorder. These are children who demonstrate egocentrism as the main trait, or those who exhibit distorted thinking. For instance, they might misinterpret an event, seeing hostility as another's intention.

ADHD

Children who have ADHD often suffer from ODD. This is because they already have the terrain for the manifestations associated with this disorder, being easily distracted and impulsive. Their behavior is often in contrast with the expectations of parents, caregivers and authority figures. Studies have confirmed that 30-50% of children with ADHD also suffer from oppositional defiant disorder.

Such children may find it difficult, if not impossible, to stay in one place, constantly going from one activity to the other. Parents will often see their behavior as a lack of discipline, transmitting negative feedback. The response coming from them will reinforce the vicious cycle, affecting their child's behavior and aggravating the manifestations of ODD.

It can also happen that adults, upon seeing their children behave in this manner, will stop any kind of discipline. They may become excessively permissive, doing their best to accommodate the demands of their children. This is done from the desire to maintain a peaceful family atmosphere, but it can cause a lot of damage in the long run.

CHAPTER 3 – AT WHAT AGE CAN OPPOSITIONAL DEFIANT DISORDER BE DIAGNOSED?

The diagnosis of ODD is not made with ease, as the condition often overlaps with other developmental disorders or mental health issues. Thus, it can be difficult to establish which manifestations are exclusively caused by oppositional defiant disorder.

As a general rule, the earliest a diagnosis of oppositional defiant disorder could be made is around the age of four. Up to the age of three, it is part of normal development for children to exhibit oppositional and defiant behaviors. They are seeking independence, discovering the power of saying "no" and testing the limits of parents, caregivers or educators.

It falls to an experienced child psychiatrist or developmental psychologist to determine whether the behavior of a child is age-appropriate or extreme. For the diagnosis of ODD to be made, one must demonstrate a recurrent behavioral pattern for at least six months, including an angry or irritable mood, argumentative or defiant behavior, and vindictiveness. The behavior must involve at least one other person, including those outside the family.

Children of a young age, usually under three, often have temper tantrums. These resemble some of the manifestations of oppositional defiant disorder, and this is the reason the diagnosis process is often delayed. One must remember that these tantrums are age-appropriate behavior and should not be interpreted as ODD.

In the majority of the cases, the condition is diagnosed upon finishing pre-school or when the child is just starting elementary school.

Mental health professionals will perform a comprehensive evaluation to make an accurate diagnosis. They will take into account the fact that the condition appears simultaneously with other behavioral issues, seeking to make the distinction between the associated manifestations.

What does the evaluation entail?

The assessment will consider the overall health of the child, with special attention being given to the manifestations suggestive of ODD (frequency, intensity, and timeframe). The specialist will inquire about the way the child behaves in different settings, including at home, school or when interacting with peers. A detailed history of the child's behavior in various settings can be useful for making an accurate diagnosis.

Family relationships will be explored during the evaluation, as the family environment can contribute to the appearance of such issues. The healthcare professional will make detailed notes on family situations, discussing strategies that have been used to manage the child's behavior. They might also discuss less helpful strategies and inquire about other mental health issues. Special tests might be needed for children who suffer from learning or communication disorders.

When making the diagnosis, the specialist will want to talk not only with the child and his/her parents, but also with other caregivers and teachers. It is important to explore every aspect of the child's behavior. Observing the child might be necessary and assessment tools are often employed for the testing of one's mental health.

If there is the suspicion that the child suffers from an underlying health condition, the psychiatrist might recommend additional investigations. Both imaging studies and blood tests can be used to diagnose underlying medical issues that may be contributing to the behavioral problem. The investigations can be useful in excluding potential causes, such as drug abuse or mental health problems.

Depending on the age of the child, direct interviews might take place. However, children are rarely capable of explaining why they behave in a certain way, especially at a younger age. They may also not understand their symptoms, with parents and caregivers being more suited to talk to. Long interviews should thus be conducted with all of the adults involved in the child's upbringing.

When should a diagnosis be sought?

One might consider getting the child evaluated for ODD if the behavioral problems, suggestive of this diagnosis, persist for over six months. A diagnosis must be sought if family dynamics are affected by the child's behavior, with other children and parents experiencing significant distress. The same goes for situations in which the child's school performance is affected, or their social interactions are limited by the behavior. If the child cannot learn, has trouble maintaining friendships or is at risk of harm, ODD might be the problem.

Tests and tools used for the diagnosis

The Diagnostic and Statistical Manual of Mental Disorders (DSM-5), established and published by the American Psychiatric Association, includes specific diagnostic criteria for oppositional defiant disorder in children. Based on these criteria, the condition can range from mild to severe. The checklist in the DSM should always be compared to the behavior of the child, including direct answers from him/her (if old enough).

The Anxiety Disorder Interview Schedule is a structured interview, in which both the parent and the child answer questions regarding such mental health issues. The specialist might also resort to the Eyberg Child Behavior Inventory, which is completed by the parent and assesses the behavior of the child.

Another potential tool used for diagnosis is the Child Behavior Checklist, which is also filled in by the parent and contains specific sections that can be used for the assessment of suspected oppositional defiant disorder. Last, but not least, the Parental Stress Index can be used to determine how stressed the parent is, following the child and his/her behavior, other adults and life events.

The earlier the diagnosis is made, the sooner an intervention plan can be created and the child's behavior improved. Parents who suspect that their children might suffer from ODD should not delay going to a specialist, as only a trained professional can make an accurate diagnosis and recommend the most effective intervention strategies.

CHAPTER 4 – DOES BAD PARENTING CAUSE OPPOSITIONAL DEFIANT DISORDER?

Parents are often worried that their child-rearing skills may have contributed to the appearance of oppositional defiant disorder. This is a frivolous way to look at things; in reality, the matter is much more complex. From the start, it should be mentioned that, even though bad parenting can be a contributing factor, it cannot lead to ODD on its own. The whole picture includes additional aspects, many of which have been mentioned in the previous chapter.

Temperamental children feel most comfortable when a conflict has arisen, but parents must remember that the way they respond in this situation can make a huge difference. One should not choose a certain way to behave, just because other family members consider "bad parenting" to be the main issue.

A parent who offers inconsistent discipline can contribute to the development of oppositional defiant disorder. Matters can be made worse by the fact that the discipline strategies one would normally use on a child will not work in the case of a temperamental, defiant or oppositional child. In reality, the problem is often complicated not by "bad parenting" but rather, "ineffective" parenting.

What does ineffective parenting refer to?

Each child is born with his/her own personality, as well as temperament. While some children are quite easy to bring up and educate, others will pose difficulties and demand more attention from their parents.

Unfortunately, when it comes to difficult children, parents rarely choose to be calm and calculated. Their own experiences, especially as a child, will often dictate their behavior as parents. In the majority of cases, parents opt for coerciveness; they are harsh with their children, with neglect and/or abuse often following as a result.

These parenting techniques are not only ineffective but they will cause the child to experience difficulties in forming an attachment to his/her parents. As the child will grow up in a dysfunctional environment, he/she will have a hard time acting appropriately when interacting with other people.

When speaking with children who suffer from oppositional defiant disorder, many specialists discover that their parents are aggressive regularly. They often resort to corporal punishment or verbal abuse, trying to keep the behavior of the child under control and get things back to "normal."

How does a stressed parent fit into the picture?

Parents can be stressed for various reasons. They might feel insecure about their parenting skills, have a lot of work to do or be dealing with marital conflicts. Stress plays a significant role in family dynamics, contributing to early developmental stress and increasing the risk of ODD.

When dealing with chronic stress, a parent will often opt for ineffective parenting practices. Abuse, neglect and inconsistent discipline may be chosen in place of a calm, organized approach. As a result, the child will respond, opting for oppositional and defiant behavior. The vicious cycle must be broken through adequate intervention, with both the parent and child changing their behavior.

Are parents always to blame?

The answer is no. Parents might blame themselves for the way a child behaves but this is not always the case. Temperamental children know exactly which buttons to push, taking advantage of the immediate stress-related response the parent provides. Parents will often experience desperation, especially upon realizing that the parental strategies they were familiar with are not effective when dealing with a non-neurotypical child.

As a parent, one must remember that emotions can take over, leading to their response to the child's behavior being inadequate. One must not give in to the child's behavior out of fear or desperation. Moreover, sometimes the child's behavior cannot be controlled and parents must learn to not associate such situations with "bad parenting."

Dysfunctional families

A dysfunctional family is one in which the relationships between parents and children are mostly defined by conflict, criticism or even abuse. The quality of family life remains one of the most important factors in the development of oppositional defiant disorder.

Poor parenting skills increase the risk of disruptive behaviors. Children who are inadequately supervised, those who are offered inconsistent education or are rejected by their parents, are most likely to develop ODD. The same goes for situations involving physical and/or verbal abuse, neglect, conflict or violence.

Negative parenting practices are almost always associated with repeated parent-child conflicts. Living in a dysfunctional family, the child will not be able to adjust to life outside the vicious cycle. He/she will struggle, having formed insecure attachments. The weak bond with one or both parents is often made worse by family instability, such as in the case of uninvolved parents, or in cases of divorce or separation.

What does bad parenting entail?

There are certain things that parents do which can qualify as "bad parenting." Parents need to recognize these habits and correct their behavior, as this will help the child be less defiant and/or oppositional.

Some parents may have gotten used to reprimanding their child regularly, even when he/she has acknowledged his/her mistakes. The parent must think back to his/her childhood and understand that it takes a lot of courage to be honest. Also, it is never a good thing to punish or scold the child in front of other people, as this will only lead to feelings of shame and the behavior will never improve.

Children consider their parents to be pillars of support. For this reason, they need to receive less advice and be encouraged more. While it is perfectly fine to direct the child and teach him/her how things should be done, it is not acceptable to stick only on this lane. Children need plenty of encouragement while growing up, and using positive words will never cause damage.

Lack of affection does count as bad parenting. Children whose parents do not display an adequate amount of affection will often be characterized as naughty. This is because they are willing to do anything to get the parent's attention, whether it is positive or negative. In this situation, we are talking about a child who needs his/her parent to be more affectionate and have a stronger emotional connection.

Smaller versions of ourselves, children require support in all aspects of life, but especially during hard times. If parents are not supportive when children are going through a difficult moment, such as getting an undeserved bad grade, their behavior might reflect it. Children often feel neglected when parents concentrate on other things.

A parent who is always comparing his/her child to another also fails at their job. It is not a bad thing to present your child with a role model, but the constant comparison is not healthy. It will place the child under immense pressure, and increase the risk of opposition, defiance and so on.

Matters are made even worse when it comes to parents who are never proud of their children's achievements. Children need to feel appreciated, just like adults. A parent with a critical tone can cause real damage, forcing the child to engage in inadequate behaviors. One should always find the time to hear and understand what the child has to say.

Children need to be taken seriously. As parents, we are responsible for setting an example and we must remember that children often mirror our habits. A child will not suffer from ODD just because we are bad parents, but this is a definite influence to take into consideration. And we should take the necessary measures to correct our behavior before it is too late.

CHAPTER 5 – HOW TO IDENTIFY THE CAUSE – A SYMPTOM OF A DEEPER ISSUE

T Oppositional defiant disorder includes several obvious behaviors, with the child being angry or irritable all the time, exhibiting defiance or even trying to seek revenge. Simultaneously, the child might experience social distress, and the family and other people can be affected by disruptive behavior.

In many cases, the condition co-exists with other mental health issues. Children with ODD can also suffer from anxiety, depression, learning disabilities and ADHD. It is essential to address these mental health disorders, as this will improve the ODD manifestations as well.

Mental health specialists have the responsibility of looking at the big picture, trying to identify the deeper issues behind oppositional defiant disorder. If mental health issues are not properly assessed and treated, the behavior of the child will only get worse.

It is also important to understand that children with co-morbid disorders will always pose temperamental challenges, in the sense that they become angry more easily and have difficulty reaching a calm state. They are prone to disruptive behavior, due to the permanent presence of negative emotions and pessimism. Of course, these traits are often aggravated by dysfunctional family life, with its excessive punishment and negative reinforcement.

ODD and anxiety

Oppositional defiant disorder can be present in children who already suffer from anxiety. It has been suggested that the anxiety disorder can overlap with ODD, causing symptoms of both to be exacerbated. Research has identified dysfunctions of the limbic system and the prefrontal cortex in children who suffer from both these disorders.

Children who are diagnosed with anxiety disorder react more easily to stimuli and are quick to place blame on other people, even when it comes to their own behavior. On the other hand, children with ODD may tend towards aggression, seeking to blame others as well. Moreover, they will expect their behavior – whether positive or negative – to bring their desired outcome in every case.

The combination of ODD and anxiety can increase the risk of misinterpretation of social cues. Such children often give in to negative emotions, they react quickly and aggressively; they present emotional dysregulation and poor inhibition control. Children who cannot regulate their emotions are more likely to be angry, irritable or frustrated, especially when their requests or demands fail to be met.

Negative interaction with one or both parents, as well as with peers, can make disruptive behavior worse. This is connected to the fact that these children are not taught strategies for the adequate regulation of their emotions. The lack of an adaptive behavior to model can add to the problem.

ODD and depression in adolescents

Adolescents who suffer from depression might have manifestations characteristic of oppositional defiant disorder. Studies have confirmed that the treatment recommended for depression, consisting of medication and cognitive behavioral therapy, could also be beneficial for the ODD symptoms.

Depression is one of the most common mental health issues in adolescents, associated not only with emotional issues, but also with behavioral and social ones. If oppositional defiant disorder is also present, functional impairment is increased. This can be reflected in school performance and peer relationships.

Adolescents who have both depression and ODD are often irritable, they might seek to hurt others and oppose the demands/requests of their parents. Cognitive behavioral therapy usually provides better results than medication. Mental health professionals should take into account the possibility of ODD when considering potential treatment solutions for adolescents who suffer from depression.

In making the diagnoses of depression and ODD, the specialist should take into account the quality of family life, major life events and the influence of the environment on the associated manifestations. There might also be specific cognitive and social factors that maintain such mental health issues, so these should be addressed as well.

ODD and ADHD

Oppositional defiant disorder is a behavioral issue, while ADHD is a neurodevelopmental disorder. These are different conditions but they can occur together. ADHD can make the symptoms of ODD more noticeable, and the other way around. The two conditions tend to build on each other, and can lead to complex disruptive behavior.

A child with ADHD will have high energy levels, becoming easily excited by even the simplest stimuli. He/she might be too rough with his/her peers, sometimes causing unintended harm to others. Tantrums can be present and, because of ODD, impulse control is reduced. Such children are often angry and irritable, sometimes being aggressive, both verbally and physically.

Research has confirmed a connection between ODD and ADHD, especially concerning impulse control. In some cases, children will misbehave, but not intentionally. The opposition appears as they are not able to control their impulses.

It has also been suggested that ODD might be a coping strategy in children with ADHD, allowing them to deal with the frustration and emotional pain experienced. Additional influencing factors to consider include genetics, family life, environment, and psychological changes.

ODD and learning disabilities

Children with intellectual disabilities present a higher risk of disruptive behaviors. Lower cognitive abilities are associated with a significant rate of conduct disorders later on in life. Such children might also suffer from language impairment and reduced verbal intelligence. The presence of ODD can lead to additional struggles, especially when it comes to learning and information processing.

CHAPTER 6 – UNDERSTANDING THE DANGER OF UNTREATED OPPOSITIONAL DEFIANT DISORDER

When it comes to oppositional defiant disorder, early intervention will lead to the best outcome. The problematic behavior needs to be adequately managed, with therapy concentrating on improving the relationship between parents and children (positive family interactions).

No treatment equals worse behavior

By starting the treatment as soon as the diagnosis has been made, parents can correct the worrying behavior and prevent the condition from becoming worse, or turning into a more serious disorder.

If no treatment measures are taken, the child suffering from ODD might be rejected by his/her peers. He/she will develop poor social skills, making him/her aggressive and irritating. There is always the risk of him/her developing a conduct disorder, which can be accompanied by more severe behavior. Such children or teens might take parts in criminal acts, hurting others, lighting fires or stealing.

By improving the relationship between the parents and the child, the entire family dynamic will change for the better. From a different perspective, getting specialized help is essential for the child's future. Behavioral issues of this kind can prevent one from forming healthy relationships, not to mention they will continue to cause a tense atmosphere within the family.

Children who are not treated for ODD have a reduced chance of reaching their full potential. They handle failure with difficulty, seeking to blame others when things do not go as planned. Social isolation might occur as a result, with a child making less effort to succeed academically. The behavior will take a toll on family members, with the tension damaging existing relationships.

Conduct disorder, a risk of untreated ODD

If oppositional defiant disorder is not treated in a timely manner, the child in question might develop a conduct disorder. This is a serious condition, which causes the child/teenager to break rules. He/she might run away from home or skip classes. The condition is a progressive one, in the sense that one can gradually become aggressive, either with people or animals, or in some cases, both.

Children who suffer from a conduct disorder are often bullies, getting into fights regularly. They are cruel to animals, destroy property and do not have any respect for the other people's rights. They might cause damage, either in the form of vandalism or arson. A lack of empathy dominates their behavior, combined with the inability to interpret social cues correctly.

These children/teenagers may also misinterpret another person's behavior, perceiving him/her as aggressive. They will respond aggressively in response, with fights occurring without too much effort and weapons often being involved. Animals might be hurt on purpose and property destroyed; children/teenagers suffering from this disorder often choose to throw or smash various items, or punch holes in the walls.

Lying is another common behavior for children or teenagers who suffer from ODD. They are most interested in manipulating or lying to others to get what they want or to avoid the consequences of their behavior. They might stay out late and avoid answering questions about their whereabouts. Parents often feel powerless when it comes to these conduct disorders, placing the blame on themselves.

Early treatment for a healthy adult

In very few cases, children can grow out of oppositional defiant behavior without any intervention. Nevertheless, this is not the case for the majority and only early treatment guarantees that the child or teenager will turn into a healthy, well-adjusted adult.

Studies have confirmed that teens and adults with untreated oppositional defiant disorder present a higher risk of substance abuse and depression. Parents should understand that this is not a passing phase; they are not just dealing with an angry child or a moody teenager. This is a mental health issue and it should be addressed, to reduce the risk of conduct disorder, antisocial personality disorder and other unhealthy behaviors.

About half of children with untreated oppositional defiant disorder will exhibit the same behavior later in life, research has confirmed. Moreover, another half will most likely develop conduct disorder.

Ignoring ODD will not make it go away

As a parent, you cannot hope for the ODD manifestations to go away on their own. You cannot stay idle and ignore what is happening. If no measures are taken, the child's academic performance might be affected. Apart from that, he/she might be subjected to disciplinary action, being suspended or expelled.

Academic failure is a huge risk in these situations and it can lead to him/her have difficulties getting or maintaining a job in later life. Such people have a hard time developing and maintaining healthy relationships, finding it impossible to positively engage with peers, colleagues, etc. Isolation can be a consequence of untreated or ignored ODD, and one might often run into trouble with the law.

Without treatment, one might begin to suffer from low self-esteem, with depression and anxiety appearing as a result. They may wonder about their sense of self-worth, and might engage in behaviors that are either dangerous or risky. They will have to suffer the consequences of these behaviors and, in return, may turn to negative solutions to feel better, such as alcohol or drug abuse. Self-harm is a major complication, and one might entertain suicidal ideas. The most important thing to remember is that it is never too late to intervene and help someone who suffers from ODD.

You've read above that some children outgrow this behavior. We are talking about a very small percentage of children, who have understood that their behavior is not appropriate and are making a conscious effort to change for the better. However, even in these situations, there is always the risk of the fire remaining dormant and the behavior resurfacing years later.

The best solution is to address the problematic behavior from the start, getting to the root cause and equipping the child with effective strategies for a behavior that is healthy and appropriate. Of course, individual circumstances play an important role in how everything will turn out. Parents, once again, have the responsibility of closely monitoring the behavior of their child/teenager and taking him/her to a mental health specialist as soon as concerns have been raised.

CHAPTER 7 – CHILD VERSUS TEENAGER – DIFFERENT BEHAVIORS, DIFFERENT APPROACHES

ODD in children

Parents are used to their children acting out. But when one begins to notice a pattern of misbehavior over an extended period of time, the problem might go deeper. Oppositional defiant disorder causes children to become angrier and more irritable than normal. They might easily lose their temper and have trouble following the requests of parents or other authority figures.

Children who suffer from an oppositional defiant disorder will argue with adults, refusing to comply with their demands and doing their best to create annoyance. They will place the blame for their behavior on other people, as well as seeking revenge. The behavior will be present for at least six months, affecting social or academic performance, and creating tension within the family.

When parenting a child with ODD, you have to think about the consequences of misbehavior, as behavioral issues can seriously interfere with healthy development. Repeated patterns of negative interactions can aggravate ODD but, at the same time, they can set the terrain for a teen who suffers from more serious issue, such as conduct disorder.

It is a well-known fact that children with ODD thrive on conflict. Master manipulators, even though not always with intention, they know how to push the right buttons and create conflict with their parents. Once this happens, they will feel in control and enjoy the sense of power derived from the conflict. Parents, on the other hand, will question themselves and their abilities to parent the child.

Perhaps the most important thing to remember is that typical punishment never work with a child who suffers from the oppositional defiant disorder. They argue as effectively as a lawyer and, even though a consequence might create discomfort, they will find ways to get around. The first thing that a parent should do is change his/her approach and think about consequences from a different perspective.

Consequences should only be used to correct a behavior and not as a form of punishment. Parents should also strive to create opportunities for positive family interactions and remember that children are going through constant development, trying to form their own identity. For a child who suffers from ODD, this process is even more difficult.

For children with oppositional defiant disorder, therapeutic solutions may include family therapy, cognitive behavioral therapy, and psychotherapy. Parent management training and social skills training might be suggested as well. What matters is that the parent is willing to make an effort to improve the relationships with his/her child, as this will be reflected in the existent behavior.

Medication is not preferred for children, as it can lead to discomforting side effects and may even fail to provide the desired result. The psychotherapist will most likely develop an individualized intervention plan, working closely with the parents to improve family relationships. In children of elementary age, parent-child interaction training might be suggested as a solution for improving behavioral issues.

ODD in teenagers

Just as small children will defy their parents in an attempt to form their self, teenagers are highly likely to be oppositional and defiant. Preoccupied with the challenges of adolescence and trying to discover who they are and what they want to do with their life, they will resist any attempt to be guided and, especially, controlled. This is a natural process of rebellion, with the teenager breaking away from his/her parents.

However, when this behavior is taken to the extreme, we might be talking about oppositional defiant disorder. The teenager might have suffered from ODD since an early age, but the symptoms associated with this condition were either ignored or parents simply failed to notice them. The condition can appear in adolescence as well, with no previous signs during childhood.

A teen who suffers from ODD will argue all the time, refusing to follow the rules established by his/her parents and other authority figures. As opposed to children, it can be quite harmful to place labels; the solution here is to stop concentrating on naming the situation and rather, address the root cause.

More often than with children, ODD in teens is almost always the result of a complex issue. The oppositional and defiant behavior appears as the teenager tries to hide his/her emotional pain; it presents itself as a coping strategy. Long-term trauma, abuse, and neglect have been incriminated in the appearance of such disorders in teenagers.

Teenagers who suffer from anxiety might exhibit this behavior when confronted with their fears and situations that elicit such feelings. For example, many teens deal with social anxiety, their behavior taking a negative turn when they have to take part in various activities and events. Additional conditions, such as the obsessive-compulsive disorder or various phobias, can make ODD worse.

If the teen in question has failed to form a healthy bond with his/her parents during childhood, oppositional defiant disorder might occur as a result. Insecure attachments can cause teenagers to question their self-worth; they feel like it is impossible to count on their parents, especially when it comes to being loved or cared for.

In simple terms, the behavior appears out of instinct, especially when parents try to control their child. The behavior will be triggered when the teenager is told how he/she should behave, what to think or how to feel, by parents or other authority figures. Parents, however, should understand that this is an instinctive reaction, which appears without one's intention and is related to the need to form one's own identity.

Frequent emotional outbursts can characterize the behavior of such a teenager. He/she might feel less motivated to complete school assignments, showing either passivity or procrastination. Parents may notice a lack of respect, a negative attitude, and/or resistance to fulfilling demands.

The teen might become easily annoyed and frustrated. Not only will he/she question the rules but he/she will refuse to follow them. Arguments with parents are common, with the teenager being irritated and even spiteful.

As you might have understood, there are certain differences between the behavior of a child and a teenager who suffers from ODD. In teenagers, psychotherapy and parent training are preferred, while medication is recommended for more severe cases. It is also essential to treat co-morbid disorders and teach parents the right strategies to stay connected with their children, regardless of their age.

CHAPTER 8 – BRAIN DEVELOPMENT

It is believed that oppositional defiant disorder might be caused by brain defects. The behavioral condition has been linked to imbalanced brain chemicals – neurotransmitters – which contribute to healthy communication between various regions. The lack of balance can impair this communication, leading to manifestations specific to ODD.

Another theory suggests that oppositional defiant disorder appears as a result of retained primitive reflexes, with the lower brain development being incomplete. Children who get in arguments frequently, with temper tantrums being part of their daily behavior, might have a retained Moro reflex.

This leads to a permanent "flight-or-fight" response, with significant quantities of adrenaline and cortisol being released regularly. What does this mean? The child in question is always prepared to engage in a fight. In reality, this is only a response to the excess accumulation of stress hormones.

But the parent only sees a child who refuses to comply with demands or requests. This is a child whose brain is not wired like the brains of other children – in fact, some automatic functions might be missing, preventing the brain from being organized.

Let's look at an example to better understand the brain issues associated with ODD. A child who refuses to get dressed will be perceived as oppositional and defiant, especially if this occurs quite frequently. However, in reality, the brain might send signals to the body that the fabric in question is uncomfortable. Tags might also be an issue.

This is because certain parts of the brain (the midbrain) are not well developed.

Parents must be educated to understand that the refusal to get dressed is not an act of opposition or defiance. It is rather the reaction the brain has determined when confronted with the situation in question. We are talking about a disorganized brain, and such children often find life more manageable when they are in control, even when it comes to something that may seem trivial, such as getting dressed.

The act of refusal, no matter its consequences, will provide one with a sense of control. Children with ODD feel empowered when they see others losing their nerve. They thrive on conflict, looking for negativity and resentment; they seek to blame others for things that do not go according to plan or for personal mistakes. All of these are the result of a disorganized brain, and they represent coping strategies.

You can imagine how frustrating it would be to lack the capacity to function normally. This is one of the reasons children who suffer from oppositional defiant disorder can be vindictive and spiteful. They are intelligent and it does not take a lot for them to realize they are different.

Inadequate processing of punishment

In analyzing the brains of children who have ODD, researchers have discovered that the amygdala has a reduced reactivity to negative stimuli. Moreover, the transmission of noradrenalin and serotonin is compromised. Fear conditioning is impaired and reactivity to stress is reduced.

All of these neurological changes translate into inadequate processing of punishment. Both children and teenagers who suffer from oppositional defiant disorder are unable to make the connection between their inappropriate behavior and the punishment that might follow.

Reduced interest in rewards

Most children are willing to correct their behavior when offered various rewards. In children with ODD, it has been discovered that the reactivity to incentives is reduced, this being connected to the inadequate functioning of the sympathetic nervous system. They do not seek the pleasant sensations associated with rewards, with the orbitofrontal cortex being hyporeactive and the dopamine function altered.

As their behavior cannot be improved through rewards or incentives, children and teenagers with ODD will try to get rid of the unpleasant sensations they are experiencing by engaging in destructive behaviors. They might break rules, skip school or run away from home. Delinquency and substance abuse might also occur as a result.

Reduced control over emotions

The executive function of the brain is impaired in children and teenagers with ODD – this is also a clear sign that they cannot be easily motivated to change their behavior. Studies have confirmed a structural deficit associated with the inadequate functioning of the paralimbic system.

The orbitofrontal cortex, as well as the cingulate cortex, do not function as they should when it comes to oppositional defiant disorder. This means that cognitive control is reduced, especially when it comes to the ability to keep one's emotions in check. In simple terms, it is difficult to control emotional behavior and stay within the norm.

Associated conditions & brain abnormalities

In studies performed on children and teenagers who suffer from ODD, in combination with a conduct disorder, it has been demonstrated that the brain presents structural abnormalities. These concern the frontal lobe, insula, and amygdala in particular.

In children with ODD and ADHD, the brain has a reduced volume, this being especially seen in areas responsible for making decisions, staying attentive and retaining information (working memory). Both frontal lobes have a reduced volume, which suggests the impairment of cognitive functioning.

Imaging studies can be used to identify brain abnormalities in children who are suspected to be suffering from ODD. Such investigations are important, as they can determine the areas in which brain functions are impaired. The results of CT scans and MRIs can guide the therapy in the right direction.

CHAPTER 9 – THEY ARE NOT ALL THE SAME – KNOW YOUR CHILD'S PATTERNS

T Oppositional defiant disorder is diagnosed, in the majority of cases, based on symptoms included in the DSM-5. Unfortunately, as most parents notice, the symptom count matters more than the individual symptom pattern.

Even though children who suffer from ODD might present similar symptoms, parents must make an effort to understand that each child will present a unique symptom pattern. The current diagnostic criteria are indeed useful for concluding that one's child has oppositional defiant disorder, but one should refrain from thinking that all children with ODD are the same.

Your child has a unique symptom profile

As a parent, you know your child best. Upon receiving the diagnosis of ODD, it is only normal to pay attention to the symptoms specific to this condition. However, you should go the extra length and think not only about checking the number of symptoms, but also which symptoms are present.

Why is it so important to pay attention to your child's unique symptom profile? The answer is simple. The only way to correct his/her behavior is through individualized intervention. And you cannot provide this kind of therapy if you think about your child in the same way as others. Moreover, this individual pattern will help you identify the riskiest behaviors in your child, which might contribute to the disorder being present in teenaged years and even during adulthood.

Monitor your child regularly

Parents – mothers, in particular – have incredible instincts. They almost always know when something is not right with their child. Some mothers have reported noticing the abnormal behavior from an early age. Such children are often described as "rigid" and "demanding," with parents complaining of specific manifestations from a very young age.

They see their child talking back all the time, refusing to comply with demands or using offensive language. The oppositional and defiant attitude might not be present in their mind as a disorder, but they know that action must be taken.

Even before the diagnosis of ODD is made, parents should monitor their children/teenagers regularly. This will help them determine their child's individual pattern, and also determine whether this is something that occurs occasionally or frequently. There are always days when the child seems at his/her worst, but this does not mean there is an actual disorder to worry about. However, when a negative pattern is noticed over an extended period, it might be the right time to visit a specialist.

What is your child's pattern?

To determine your child's pattern, you need to be familiar with all of the manifestations that could fall under oppositional defiant disorder. Is your child uncooperative, refusing for example to do chores? Does he/she display defiance and hostility? In answering these questions, you will be one step closer to acknowledging the presence of ODD and the way it interferes with your child's daily functioning.

Your child or teen might argue excessively, with temper tantrums being a common occurrence. He/she might be actively defiant, refusing to comply with your demands. Efforts will be made to annoy parents and other authority figures; these are the children/teenagers who thrive on upsetting others. They will not hesitate to blame other people for the way they behave or when making mistakes. Touchy and easily annoyed, they will also seek revenge.

Early identification of one's pattern is important

Not all parents are willing to accept that their child has a problem. Despite confronting negative behavior daily, they will look the other way and avoid facing the problem. Unfortunately, time passes and the child will soon become a teenager, at risk of developing a conduct disorder.

Even though it might be difficult, it is important to get to the root of the problem early on. It is far easier to identify the unique pattern of behavior during childhood so that therapy can be started. If one waits until the teenaged years, it will be quite difficult to reach this diagnosis. In most cases, the condition is confused with normal adolescent rebellion.

Recognizing a teenager with ODD

Parents might be struggling to determine whether their teenager suffers from oppositional defiant disorder or if he/she is just being a rebel. The key is to pay attention to their daily behavior, noticing how intense the rebellion is and how much hostility is involved in the process.

Once again, parents must be educated concerning adequate teenager behavior and normal development. However, you should refrain from constantly comparing your teen his/her peers, as this habit might raise the wrong questions.

Parenting a child/teen with ODD

In the following chapters, we will discuss how parents should deal with a child or teenager who suffers from such a disorder. In the meantime, try to remember that the child/teen should be monitored in both home and school settings. Negative interactions should be identified and corrected.

Raising a child/teen with ODD can be frustrating and exhausting. One thing that can help is understanding that your child/teen is unique. His/her behavior can be managed with some effort. Parents must be consistent in their behavior, and understand that it is a unique challenge to raise a child or teenager who suffers from such a disorder.

Traditional parenting techniques might not work, as one constantly faces opposition and defiance. It takes practice to discover the techniques that will work with your child, and probably just as much patience. Regardless of their behavior, children should not be deprived of unconditional love and they should be accepted for who they are. Remember, both children and teenagers need to be loved the most when they are not at their best.

Parents should also refrain from being too hard on themselves. It is difficult to parent a child/teen with ODD, but once you accept that he/she needs help overcoming this challenging behavior, it will be easier to see the light ahead. A lot of energy should be put into improving the relationship with the child and helping him/her manage strong emotions.

It is normal to hope and believe that the child/teen will outgrow the challenging behavior on his/her own. However, in most cases, the condition will not disappear just because you hoped for this to happen. The child/teenager requires professional diagnosis and individualized intervention as soon as possible.

Your child is a unique individual and you should love him/her unconditionally. Oppositional defiant disorder is just a part of him/her and the behavior can be improved with the right treatment. Always let your child or teenager know that he/she is important to you, and do your best to spend plenty of positive time together.

CHAPTER 10 – HOW DO YOU DEAL WITH AN OPPOSITIONAL DEFIANT CHILD?

From the moment we become parents, or even sooner, we imagine how our children will grow and develop. However, when it comes to a child who suffers from a behavioral disorder such as ODD, the reality might not match our expectations. This can lead to a lot of frustration, as well as disappointment.

If your child is oppositional and defiant, find the power to be patient. There are several strategies you can employ to correct his/her behavior and ensure that he/she will continue to develop healthily. Take things step by step, and do not hope for miracles. Together, chip away at the problems you are facing, doing your best to strengthen your relationship between.

Appreciate his/her positive behavior

When dealing with a child with ODD, parents tend to concentrate on the negative behavior. While this is not necessarily a mistake, it does not mean that you should disregard your child when he/she engages in positive behavior. As a good parent, you should acknowledge the effort made by the child and praise him/her accordingly.

Upon reinforcing the positive behavior of your child, you should be as specific as possible. You can show enthusiasm, but do not be more excited than normal. You might also want to hug or kiss the child, as this will add to the beneficial effect of the praise.

Be your child's role model

Manifestations associated with oppositional defiant disorder are often aggravated by negative interactions between the parent(s) and the child. If you want your child's behavior to improve, you need to model appropriate behavior.

Remember that your child looks up to you and it is your responsibility to teach him/her how things work. Demonstrate to your child how appropriate interactions take place and take your time to explain how to behave from a social point of view. You can help him/her develop social skills, as these will reduce the risk of temper tantrums.

Don't turn your relationship into a power struggle

You are the parent and thus the adult in the relationship. When conflict arises, you have to abstain from getting angry and turning your relationship into a power struggle. As the mature one, you need to pick your battles and consider whether a fight is worth pursuing or not.

Involve your child in the decision-making process

Even though children are not always able to identify the need for change in their behavior, this does not mean you should not involve them in the decision-making process. Discuss the problematic behavior and allow your child to be part of the decisions made for him/her.

You can work together on the limits to be set, making sure that your instructions are clear and effective. You might also talk about consequences, teaching your child about the situations in which these will be enforced. It is best to have these discussions without conflict, as this will guarantee the best resolution.

A routine is more than beneficial for a child with ODD

Children in general need and thrive from routine. They like to know what will happen next and feel confused when things do not go according to plan. A well-established routine gives them the sensation that they are in control, a sensation which is just as much appreciated by a child with ODD.

Do your best to develop and respect a daily schedule for your child. Depending on his/her age, you might involve him/her in the activities to be included in the schedule. Children appreciate such responsibilities and, given they are allowed to decide, they might find it easier to be on their best behavior.

Time together equals better behavior

Children need their parents. You need to spend time together, engaging in various activities that your child enjoys. Such positive interactions can counteract negative behavior, stimulating your child to behave as expected and give up on the oppositional/defiant attitude. Just remember, when spending time together, be there. Do not spend your time on the phone or distracted by other things.

All adults should follow the same disciplinary path

Once you have decided that it is time to make a change and correct the behavior of your child, everyone must follow the same path. You should work together with your partner and other caregivers, to pursue the same strategy for disciplining the child. When it comes to correcting manifestations of oppositional defiant disorder, the most important thing is to be consistent. Depending on the possibilities, you might involve other authority figures – such as teachers – in the rehabilitation process.

A household chore as a first step towards becoming responsible

You can start with a simple activity at first, one that you know your child will enjoy doing. In this way, you are setting your child up for success. Once he/she gets accustomed to completing easy-to-achieve tasks, you can add more complex household chores to the weekly schedule. Your child will learn to be responsible, concentrating on the tasks at hand rather than on his/her behavior.

Learn to say "no"

When your child is oppositional and defiant, you might have a hard time saying no. However, this word can help you correct your child's behavior. You need to be prepared for things to become worse before they get better. Your child will not appreciate you saying "no" all of a sudden, but you need to be patient.

The child will most likely resist the new expectations, with his/her negative behavior reaching new heights. You are the parent and, by remaining consistent, you will be able to challenge this behavior. Consistency remains the key to successfully dealing with such a child, so remember the power of "no" and use it at the right moment.

Find the middle ground – authority and permission

Parenthood does not come with a book. You grow as a parent, along with your child. And you might often find yourself wondering if you are doing your best. The thing to remember is that children with ODD need the best of both worlds. At times, they might need you to be authoritative and enforce limits. Other times, they will just need to be loved and held.

It is up to you, and yes it is difficult, but you should do your best to find the middle ground between being authoritative and permissive. Praise your child when necessary, opt for small rewards in case of small children and do not hesitate to provide specific instructions.

Uncooperative behavior should be addressed right away

If your child fails to comply with your demands and requests, you should address this behavior as soon as it happens. However, negative consequences should only be used as a last resort.

Let's say you have asked your child to pick up his/her toys. The child does not seem to care about your demand. You can repeat the request, once or twice. Afterward, you can mention a consequence, in the form of loss of privilege (activities, belongings).

Time out is a solution for escalating conflicts, but it should only be used when other calming strategies have failed. Older children might decide by themselves to take a time out, being aware of the need to withdraw. You should respect and support this decision, as this is clear proof of positive parenting.

Pay attention to behavioral triggers

Often, manifestations associated with oppositional defiant disorder are made worse by various triggers such as environmental and situational. You should make an effort and try to eliminate these behavioral triggers, as this will help your child behave better.

For instance, many children behave worse as a result of sleep deprivation. Make sure your child gets enough sleep, as a well-rested child will behave as expected.

Act calm and calculated

Children with oppositional defiant disorder know how to obtain the desired reaction from their parents. They use emotions to reach a negative behavior and they are indeed master manipulators. It might be difficult but you need to find the power to act calm and calculated.

When conflict arises, try to respond without anger. Do not take things personally, as your child needs you to be calm, neutral and objective. He/she will model your behavior, so make sure you are a positive example. And, most importantly, do your best to be your child's parent and not his/her friend. You are there to set limits and make sure they are followed.

CHAPTER 11 – HOW TO DISCIPLINE
A CHILD WHO DOESN'T LISTEN

A ny parent will go through moments when the child simply refuses to listen. When it comes to oppositional defiant disorder, such moments will occur more often. Frustration is a normal response but healthy parents will know that any behavior can be changed, provided the right disciplinary strategies are used.

Discipline is one thing, punishment another

Many parents confuse discipline with punishment, and this confusion will repeatedly cause the child to misbehave. Discipline is all about active involvement in the child's behavior so that you can correct negative habits. You need to be willing to put in the work, refraining from giving into anger and opting for immediate punishment.

Take your time to teach your child how to control himself/herself – restraint is not learned overnight and only repeated interactions will lead to the desired results. Punishment, by contrast, serves as a means of ensuring a direct result, but its effect is only temporary.

Punishment rarely leads to better behavior

No matter what you might think, children rarely change their behavior as a result of being punished. Parents are often tempted to resort to punishment, (erroneously) thinking that once the child has been grounded, spanked or his/her belongings have been taken, the behavior will become positive.

Even if you have taken everything away from your child and forbidden preferred activities, you might be surprised that he/she will still refuse to listen. You might be successful, in some cases, but the result will not last for long. Moreover, by adding one punishment after another, the child will simply wait for time to pass and things to get back to normal.

Children who are frequently punished not only do not change their behavior for the better, but they might make an even smaller effort to listen to their parents. As punishments occur daily, they will stop caring and continue on the trodden path. There will be no stimulus for the behavior to change and every interaction will turn into a power struggle.

Stay calm, even when you feel like exploding

In the previous chapter, we talked about the power of staying calm. When your child simply refuses to listen and you keep making demands, you might feel like you are losing control and become angry. This is the easy road to take and unfortunately the one that will cause the most damage.

Filled with anger and on the verge of exploding, you might give warnings to your child, or even go as far as to threaten him/her. We have all said phrases like "you'd better listen" or "you'd better be good." Children do not react to these statements because the information transmitted is rather vague.

The solution is to stay calm and not assume that the child knows what we want. You need to be clear and provide specific instructions, refraining from asking the impossible or setting limits that are not realistic. Otherwise, you will only become frustrated and fail to communicate with the child. A calm state prevents the child from reacting angrily or becoming overly emotional.

You are his/her parent, not his/her friend

Children who suffer from behavioral disorders such as ODD need the support of their parents, acting as authority figures and not as friends. Any child needs his/her parents but, when it comes to ODD, the need to set limits becomes even more imperative.

Parents should never be passive observers, they must be actively involved in correcting the child's behavior. You will have plenty of time, later on, to be friends; for the moment you should stick to active parenting and not hesitate to impose limits when necessary. It might be hard, but you are helping the child grow and turn into a healthy adult.

Consequences to correct behavior

Consequences represent a more effective alternative to punishments, but these should always be tied to a specific behavior. To stimulate your child to listen and change his/her behavior, you need to give the consequence right away. Remember, you want your child to learn from every experience. When privilege is restored, praise your child for the success achieved (encouragement equals a reduced chance of negative behavior in the future).

The key to success is to have only one consequence for each negative behavior. Let's say you want your child to pick up his/her toys and complete homework up to a certain hour every day. Well, if your child fails to pick up the toys, you should give a specific consequence. The same goes for failing to do his/her homework.

Do not mix consequences, as the child will get confused and the chances of success will be significantly reduced. By keeping things separate, the child will find it easier to follow through. Remember that it is in your best interest for the child to succeed. Moreover, the child needs to know that privileges earned will remain available, even when another negative behavior has occurred.

If the child seems not to care about the consequences you have given, do not be tricked. Children might act like they do not care but, in their souls, they suffer from the loss of privilege. You should not listen to what the child says but rather look at the way he/she behaves.

An effective consequence regards something important for the child. You can connect it to undesirable behavior, such as not listening to you, and offer a time frame for things to change. When privileges are earned back, the child will form an association with better behavior.

You should also be patient, as it might take some time before the consequence will work. The child might be patient as well, waiting for a few days for the privilege to be given back. He/she might act like he/she doesn't care, but you will soon see their behavior change.

Correct the behavior gradually

Children do not listen for multiple reasons. Parents, however, often try to correct everything negative about the child's behavior at once. If you have decided to make a change for the better, take things step-by-step. Work on each situation individually and move to the next only after you have been successful.

When children are given too many instructions, they can get easily overwhelmed and the last thing they will do is correct their behavior. Moreover, if you work on several levels, you might become confused yourself. Focus on the present and be patient, as children are receptive to calm approaches.

All in all, if you want your child to listen, you have to be consistent in your approach. Choose to be patient and calm, working towards positively connecting with your child.

CHAPTER 12 – HOW TO TALK TO YOUR CHILD – BEST PRACTICES

B ehavioral disorders, such as ODD, can cause a child to be difficult to talk to. Concentrated on being oppositional and defiant, the child will refuse to engage in meaningful discussions with parents, other caregivers, and/or different authority figures. Before you reach a new level of despair, there are strategies you can try, in order to connect with your child on a whole new level.

A healthy way to communicate with children

The way you talk to your child matters more than you might think. It affects his/her development, mental health and ability to listen. Parents have the responsibility of modeling the desired behavior, including when it comes to conversations.

Unfortunately, many parents nowadays opt for aggressive communication, yelling at their children, calling them names or reducing them to unimportant beings. Children are sensitive to the way parents communicate with them, acting out in response. They might develop fear as a natural response, while some will yell back and become defiant, ignoring the parents' orders.

Using an appropriate volume might be a difficult thing to achieve, as yelling comes as a natural response with a defiant child. Nevertheless, when parents yell, children stop listening. You should never engage in a yelling competition with a child. Return to the conversation only after the child has calmed down.

Passive communication is just as damaging, causing children to feel insecure and anxious. However, the more passive the parent is, the more the child will try to gain control. In some situations, the parent might reach his/her limits, with aggressiveness becoming the dominant behavior.

When it comes to healthy ways in which parents can communicate with their children, assertive communication stands at the top of the list. Parents need to be firm and consistent, giving children clear instructions, in a positive tone. They should be warm, exhibiting confidence in their own words. Children need to know that their parents are responsible adults, and their most accurate role models. Only through this type of communication, will a child learn to listen.

A calm voice goes a long way

Even when your child is disobedient, you can manage to connect with him/her by using a calm voice. Choose your words and explain, slowly and carefully, that you need him/her to do something. Do not use too many words, as the child will most likely not pay enough attention.

Keep it simple and do not give a multitude of directions, as the child will have difficulty following through. You might also consider splitting your request into smaller sections, celebrating each achievement. Always pay attention to how involved or interested is the child in the respective conversation.

Once you have stated your requirements or demands, do not pursue the issue anymore. Take yourself out of a potential argument and you will have a better chance of convincing your child to do what you asked. By engaging in conflict, on the other hand, you will give all of the power to your child and he/she will learn that defiant behavior is a successful strategy.

Not everything is negotiable

Children with ODD will defy rules and can get on your last nerve. However, their behavior can greatly improve by establishing a few rules that cannot be negotiated. Make sure these are simple to follow, to avoid overwhelming the child.

You should explain the behavior you expect to result, and the consequences associated with breaking those rules. Enforce these consequences whenever necessary and repeat the rules often. You can refer to using the right kind of language in the presence of adults, or to the fact that violence of any kind – towards people or animals – will never be allowed.

A code word for calming down

This might sound like something out of a spy book, but in reality, a code word can do a lot of good. You can let the child choose the word, for example, "cloud" or "brown" – what matters is that you are both well aware that this is a sign your child needs a time out, to calm down.

The code word can also be used for other purposes, such as when the child feels the need to express a negative emotion – anger, frustration or sadness. Parents use the word "no" too often, as well as "stop" – these are trigger words for the negative behavior, leading to a whirlwind of emotions.

Get him/her to listen by using his/her name

If your child simply refuses to listen, try saying his/her name (calmly, of course). We all like hearing our names, and children are no exception. This is a simple, yet effective method of getting their attention, so you can make a demand or request something from your child.

"Amy, can you go and get your jacket, please?" This is a powerful phrase, as it starts with the child's name. In the case of smaller children, it might be useful to say the name, then stop and wait for the child to become attentive. Once you have gotten his/her attention, you can make your request. This provides a better chance of success.

Positive language provides a better chance of success

Even though "no" might be the word you turn towards most often, remember that it will not help you be as successful as desired. Instead, opt for a positive language, clearly stating your expectations.

It might take some practice to eliminate or reduce "no" from your vocabulary but the effort will be worth it. Avoid ridiculing the child ("you're acting like a big baby"), calling him/her names ("you idiot") or saying that you are disappointed or ashamed of him/her. Not only will this kind of language make ODD manifestations worse, but the child's self-esteem will suffer. As a result, communication between the two of you will become even more difficult.

When you speak in a positive tone and choose kind words, the child will respond with confidence. He/she will be happy to talk to you, with his/her behavior improving as a result. Positive language serves as encouragement for children, stimulating them to try harder to change and be successful in their endeavors. Remember that children imitate us, including the way we speak and the words we use. Do not be afraid to say "I like that you did...", "Thank you for...", "I am happy you tried..." The results will be impressive, to say the least.

Eye contact at every conversation

A simple way to connect with your child is to establish eye contact. You should get down to their level and demonstrate that you are interested in talking to them. You may sit at the table with your child, demonstrating impeccable manners and helping them to listen.

As mentioned above, it is useful to say the child's name, as this will help you obtain the desired eye contact. This is particularly important if you are interested in requesting something from your child. Eye contact ensures they are attentive and, at the same time, it is a sign that you are genuinely concerned about their person.

Gentle but firm

When talking to your child, you need to be gentle but firm. If you have made a request, do not go back on it. You need to keep your ground and add significance to the demand in question. Speak with confidence and do not hesitate, otherwise the child will get the impression that you are not that interested in him/her complying.

Children are not easy beings to talk to, especially when they also have a behavioral issue, such as oppositional defiant disorder. Nevertheless, by practicing the art of talking, and resorting to the aforementioned mentioned strategies, you will manage to establish a connection. Just make sure that you seek out your child and engage in meaningful conversations, enjoying the time spent together.

CHAPTER 13 – HOW TO CREATE HEALTHY BOUNDARIES – WINNING STRATEGIES FOR WORKING WITH YOUR CHILD

B oundaries are necessary for children, as they teach them to be respectful and follow the rules set by parents. When establishing boundaries, parents might face a series of challenges, especially since children with ODD thrive on pushing these boundaries every day.

The truth is that children, in general, have the energy and natural desire to push us, permanently testing our limits. When it comes to oppositional defiant disorder, matters are made even worse. Nevertheless, with the right measures, it is possible to create and maintain healthy boundaries, improving the relationship with the child and his/her behavior in general.

A clear definition of boundaries

If you want to be successful, you need to clearly define the desired boundaries. The child must be fully aware of your values, the thoughts you have concerning respect and your position when it comes to overcoming those boundaries. The clearer you are, the easier it will be for him/her to adapt to the newly-created situation.

Of course, it is not always easy to define boundaries. It might need some practice and a lot of patience on your part. It is also essential that you do not become too rigid, otherwise the child will become even more defiant and oppositional.

Choose a quiet period to talk about these boundaries, being honest throughout the entire conversation. Children value honesty above all else and they always imitate their parents. Keep in mind that your actions often play a more significant role than your words. You should respect boundaries as well.

Come clean about your expectations

As mentioned in the previous chapter, children respond well to expectations that are laid out clearly, including when it comes to boundaries. Make your demands known and tell them what is acceptable, and what you cannot tolerate. Teach them to be responsible and respect boundaries, even when they feel like this is an impossible thing to achieve.

Even if you are dealing with a child who suffers from oppositional defiant disorder, this does not mean you should have absurd expectations. You are meant to help your child correct his/her behavior, but not to take complete control.

Respect yourself and the child will model your behavior

A sound principle to teach your child with ODD is respect. You might be upset that he/she is frequently disobedient, using aggressive language. Every time this behavior occurs, do not hesitate to present him/her with a specific consequence. Gradually, your child will see that you value respect and become more accountable for his/her actions.

Your child might misbehave, refusing to listen to you. This is the right time to focus on yourself and try to model the behavior you want the child to adopt. Communicate that you value respect and active listening, and hold your child accountable for failing to respond properly.

Discuss the impact of a crossed boundary

Sometimes parents expect children to understand things at an adult level. However, this is simply not possible and one should keep in mind that children develop at their own pace and it takes a long time before they reach maturity. Children will cross boundaries, offering you the perfect opportunity to discuss the impact of misbehavior.

By bringing this discussion to light, you are drawing attention to the fact that crossing boundaries comes with specific consequences. You should support the child in acknowledging the mistake made and even apologizing. Children with ODD might learn to respect boundaries through repeated experiences. It is only with practice that they will learn to respect limits and, thus, you as a parent.

Trustworthiness, a quality children value in their parents

You expect your child to trust you, and your abilities as a parent. Nonetheless, you should remember that children have similar expectations. They need to know that they count on their parents, expecting words to always be backed up by actions.

If you are not trustworthy, children will detach from the relationship and ODD manifestations will become worse. Moreover, as your words will lose their meaning, it will be close to impossible to establish boundaries and have these respected.

Verify that the child has understood the message transmitted

Miscommunication is one of the main reasons parents often fail to impose boundaries. You want to set limits within a positive environment, so you should do your best to communicate effectively.

Once you have discussed the new boundaries, you might want to ask your children to repeat what has been said. In this way, you will verify that the child has understood the message transmitted. You are doing a simple thing, but one that will guarantee everyone is on the same page.

Depending on the age of the child, you might also want to involve the child in setting boundaries. You can organize a family meeting and make sure every member gets a say. In this way, the children will appreciate being perceived as responsible and will do their best to improve their behavior, respecting the boundaries you have created. Appropriate behavior should always be recognized and appreciated. Many parents, unfortunately, pay more attention to boundaries being violated rather than respected.

No labels – concentrate on limits instead

It is easy for a parent to lose his/her temper, placing different labels on the child. Children interiorize these attributes, perceiving themselves as "bad," "naughty" or "disruptive." If you want ODD manifestations to tone down, stop labeling your child. Instead, concentrate on the boundaries you want to impose.

When you tell a child he/she has been bad, this will not have a positive effect on his/her behavior. On the contrary, it will only reinforce the negative self-image. The better solution would be to talk about limits – what is "acceptable" and what is "unacceptable."

You should also allow your child to express his/her own opinion, provided he/she is respectful and kind. Go over the rules of having a discussion, and make sure these are respected while talking about boundaries. Older children might have the courage to say that a certain boundary is not fair and you have to listen to the stated opinion. Together, you might be able to reach a better resolution.

Perhaps the most important thing is that you are consistent when it comes to boundaries imposed. Do not change your mind about a specific boundary, as you will send the message that limits can be broken and that respect does not matter as much as it should.

Children with ODD need time to process and acknowledge the presence of boundaries. They might need to be reminded about existent boundaries and the consequences that will result from breaking the set rules. Practice makes perfect and you should always be there for your child, helping him/her understand what he/she is supposed to do and how.

CHAPTER 14 – OVERCOMING OBSTACLES

When we are expecting a child, we spend a lot of our time thinking about how our little wonder will turn out. As the child grows, it is only normal to expect him/her to do as we ask. Nonetheless, when behavioral issues complicate our existence, it can be genuinely frustrating to deal with the child and his/her temper tantrums.

Parents are not born with the skills to deal with oppositional or defiant behavior but they learn these when faced with the challenge. The key to overcoming the obstacles associated with ODD, and helping the child become a functional adult, is to see beyond the behavior.

By re-thinking some of the solutions you have used in the past to manage your child's behavior, you might be successful in reducing the resistance associated with different activities or tasks. Follow our strategies to turn your relationship into a fruitful one, eliminating stress and frustration.

Pay attention to your behavior just as much

We all have our ways of dealing with a child's undesirable behavior, and these might not be the most effective solutions (especially when it comes to punishment). By stubbornly sticking to old ways, we will only reinforce negative interactions and increase the child's resistance to change.

So, we need to pay attention to our own behavior, just as much as we do to the behavior of the child. We want the child to feel stimulated to change and, as previously mentioned, power struggles are never the way to go. They will only place the child in control of the situation; as soon as they receive a negative response, they will become more defiant and oppositional.

Learn how to make a request or demand

Parents and children often end up in power struggles as a result of miscommunication. As the adult in the relationship, you have to think about how you make requests or demands – this will have a definite influence on the way your child responds, compliance-wise.

Directions should always be given clearly and directly. You have to be specific, as children do not respond well to vague indications. Use a limited amount of words and be sure to provide your child with an adequate amount of time to respond, and comply.

Refrain from unclear commands or using too many words, as the child will not be able to concentrate. Moreover, as you are looking to correct a specific behavior, stick to that. Do not provide your child with multiple instructions for various behaviors, as you will not obtain the desired effect.

Try looking at things from your child's perspective

In the book *The Little Prince*, we are reminded that "all grown-ups were once children, but only a few of them remember it." This is quite true. As parents, we tend to focus on our role, forgetting the struggles we experienced growing up. If your child exhibits resistance, you might be more successful by looking at things from his/her perspective.

The trick is to establish a connection with your child so that you can successfully communicate your message. Once the child sees that you understand from where he/she is coming from, he/she might let their guard down and allow you in. Children need to witness parents validating their points of view, as this validation will lead to compliance.

You might also want to remember that children often feed us with information on how we should successfully deal with them. When it comes to a child who suffers from oppositional defiant disorder, you might need to look harder. But the clues will still be there and it is up to you to be observant and turn these into useful strategies.

Change the context in which the behavior occurs

Resistant behavior can be changed by modifying the context in which it occurs. You are the expert and, thus, responsible for changing the setting, or the circumstances. Always remember that the context is one of the most influencing factors that determine how a child will behave.

Once the context has been changed, the child will find himself/herself in a new situation and his/her resistance will be reduced. This strategy can also be useful in helping the child feel motivated to change his/her behavior without any additional intervention.

Help the child give up the resistant behavior alone

When we see our child engaged in resistant behavior, our desire for control is activated and we immediately ask him/her to stop. What will happen? The child will refuse and continue engaging in the respective behavior. This negative interaction will send a signal that the behavior can be repeated, especially since the child thrives from the irritation seen in the parent.

A good strategy involves directing the child to engage more in resistant behavior. Even though this might not seem like a suitable idea at first, the child will not be able to tolerate the experiment for too long.

Most likely, he/she will abandon the behavior on his/her own. He/she will begin to follow your directions, engaging less and less in the undesirable behavior.

As an alternative, you can allow your child a moment in the day for the problematic behavior to occur. The child will be surprised at having the chance to freely express himself/herself. He/she will lose interest in the problematic behavior and find better ways to spend his/her time.

In the end, it is all about changing behavior and staying in control. What matters is that you do not let yourself sucked into the problematic behavior, instead finding positive ways to deal with your child's resistance. Of course, you can also visit a specialist, someone who can help your child develop coping skills and the necessary impulse control.

Overcoming obstacles in the school setting

Note: we will discuss briefly how obstacles related to ODD can be overcome in the school setting. Later, in the book, you will find an entire chapter dedicated to managing this behavioral disorder at school.

Parents should discuss with teachers opportunities for improving the child's behavior at school. A solution might be to select a seat for the child in the front of the classroom, as well as opting for structured classroom activities. It might be a good idea for the daily schedule to be displayed on a wall, so the child can feel in control about what will happen next.

With older children, teachers might organize a meeting with parents and the children themselves, to discuss potential solutions. Children might be involved in the decision-making process, so they can offer their input about improving behavior.

A special moment in the day might be dedicated to discussing emotions, as children with ODD need help managing strong emotions, such as anger and frustration. Such discussions will not only help them become less resistant, but also develop resilience.

Children should not feel punished all the time, just because they suffer from ODD and everyone concentrates on their negative behavior. Teachers should offer praise for good behavior, as this is just as the kind of positive reinforcement they need. All children should be praised for exhibiting cooperation and reduced resistance. Group sessions with other children might help improve social skills, as well as the relationship with the other schoolmates.

CHAPTER 15 – HOW TO ACT WHEN THE CHILD IS UNABLE TO IDENTIFY AND ARTICULATE HIS/HER CONCERNS

A child who suffers from a behavioral issue such as ODD will often have difficulties identifying his/her feelings. Accustomed to exhibiting resistance in front of the parent, he/she will struggle to articulate any existent concerns, interiorizing his/her true emotions.

Seeing beyond the behavior

From outside, we see a child who is defiant and oppositional. He/she is touchy and easily offended, using offensive language or seeking to blame others for his/her mistakes or misbehavior. The child with ODD is angry all the time, as well as resentful and vindictive.

Most likely, he/she will seek revenge, getting into fights with peers and refusing to comply with the demands of parents and other authority figures. The child will seek to irritate parents, other caregivers, and peers, as he/she thrives on irritating the people surrounding him/her. Temper tantrums will be frequent, especially when the child is forced to deal with a situation he/she is not comfortable with.

Parents have their unique intuition and should do their best to see beyond the negative behavior. Due to the neurodevelopmental issues, the child might suffer from anxiety, which will cause him/her to feel the constant need to be in control, of both people and his/her environment.

Acting as a responsible parent for your child

If you want your child to voice his/her concerns, you need to stay calm and use an appropriate tone. Many children with ODD see themselves as victims, so you might want to refrain from pitying your child excessively. At the same time, you have to remember that they have trouble regulating their emotions; this dysfunction is the reason sudden outbursts of anger and temper tantrums occur.

Take into consideration that your child might require a longer period to explain their behavior and associated feelings. Constructively approach the behavioral issues and allow your child to respond in his/her own time. Some children might cry as part of the process, and you should support them all the way. Once you have discussed a behavior, close the subject and do not dwell on it.

Let your child know that you are there for him/her, whenever he/she might need you. In making sure that he/she is aware of your availability, you should use both words and body language. Use direct eye contact, get down on his/her level and do not sit with your arms or legs crossed. This will be perceived as a defensive attitude, and your child will not feel free to open up. Once he/she does so, be present and listen to everything he/she has to say.

A structured environment improves behavior & offers
opportunities for seeking active communication

Children have always benefitted from a structured environment. When it comes to oppositional defiant disorder, creating such an environment matters even more. It is your responsibility as a parent to provide your child with ample opportunities for rest – both mental and physical – as well as physical exercise and adequate nutrition.

It might sound like an obvious thing to say but a child will thrive once all of these basic needs are met. Moreover, children who grow up in a structured environment – with plenty of physical activity, healthy meals and adequate amounts of sleep – can more effectively regulate their emotions.

Be empathic & understanding

Children often feel misunderstood, especially by their parents. If your child has difficulties expressing how he/she feels, do not be quick to judge. Instead, be empathetic and show your child that you understand the situation and the associated behavior.

Always try to imagine how you would have felt, had you suffered from such issues. Parents make the mistake of thinking that the feelings of children do not matter too much, as they are still not mature. In reality, children may experience the same emotions as adults, and some even more intense. Empathy will help you establish a connection with your child, encouraging him/her to speak out.

We have spoken about eye contact, as this facilitates communication between the parent and the child. When trying to get your child to come out of his/her shell, look him/her straight into the eyes. The child knows that you are his/her safe space and direct eye contact will serve as encouragement for expression. You can benefit from looking into your child's eyes as well, as children do not have a filter and you might see a lot of the emotions they are experiencing.

Children benefit from choices

If you see your child struggling to speak about his/her problems, you might want to take matters to the next level. Depending on the age of your child, present him/her with choices. Ask him/her: "Do you want to talk about what makes you angry or are you interested in speaking about the things that cause you to be anxious?"

When children are given choices, they feel like they are involved in the decision-making process. As a result of feeling empowered, they will feel more motivated to change and improve their behavior. This is such a simple way to engage your child and start a discussion.

Behave like an adult and do not belittle your child

You are the advocate for your child. As his/her parent, you should do whatever it takes for his/her behavior to improve. When parents make an effort to become involved, children feel free to express their concerns and talk about their behavior.

Do not argue with your child, as this will only make matters worse. Refrain from giving him/her long lectures, as these will be perceived as boring and the result will be anything but positive. Avoid using sarcastic remarks, offensive language or belittling your child, as this is not acceptable behavior on your part.

You should not ask your child to stop whining or threaten them with consequences for any mistake. Phrases such as "don't you dare" or "don't make me feel ashamed of you" act as triggers for negative behavior. Moreover, the child will grow up to believe he/she has reduced self-worth, seeking only negative attention.

Parents should, however, refrain from excessive encouragement. Remember that you are trying to raise a child who is balanced and resilient, capable of adjusting to a wide range of situations. When encouraging your child to express himself/herself, teach him/her that he/she should always take the needs of other people into account.

Speak about behavior as soon as it occurs

Parents should not expect children to come to them and discuss negative behavior. Children with ODD often become frustrated easily but are not necessarily able to express why they experience such feelings. If the parent doesn't intervene, things will only progress faster and the child will erupt in anger at the wrong moment.

The child might not know how to deal with frustration, and this is where the parent comes in. It is his/her job to provide the child with the skills necessary to respond to a frustrating situation in an appropriate manner. It is essential to stop trying to control the behavior of the child, and rather concentrate on reducing the possibilities for unwanted behavior. Analyze each situation and determine the associated risk accordingly.

Be open & speak about your feelings

You are your child's role model and talking about your feelings can do a lot of good. Remember that children imitate their parents, so do not be afraid to be open with your child. In this way, you will show him/her firsthand how one should express his/her feelings.

In speaking to your child about the way you feel, do not patronize him/her or show condescension. Choose your words carefully and make sure that the child understands you. Tell them about the difference between various feelings and encourage your child to ask questions, as this is an excellent opportunity for learning.

Once your child sees you opening up, he/she might find it easier to talk about his/her feelings. You can help your child label the way he/she feels, introducing common issues, such as "frustration," "anger," "sadness," "happiness" or "irritation." Teach your child that it is normal to experience such feelings and that what matters is how you deal with them.

Never teach your child to suppress his/her feelings. This is not a healthy thing to do and, long term, it will only cause the child to refrain from expressing himself/herself. When children see that parents do not accept their emotions or feelings, they develop low self-esteem and have issues adapting to real life.

CHAPTER 16 – HOW TO MANAGE
YOUR CHILD AT SCHOOL

Oppositional defiant disorder will almost always interfere with the academic performance of the child. Feeling the need to be in control all of the time, the child will test authority and push the limits. He/she might break rules, refusing to comply with demands and trying to provoke an argument, either with teachers or one of his/her peers.

Unfortunately, the presence of a child with ODD in the classroom can be distracting, not only for the students but also for the teacher. In such situations, parents need to cooperate with the teacher, finding the best strategies for behavior improvement.

What does the teacher see?

Without knowing about the child's history, the teacher will see a student who is willing to push the limits of defiance to the extreme. He/she will see a problem child, who seems angry all the time and ready to burst at the slightest provocation. Due to this overreacting, the child might have difficulties engaging in even a simple conversation.

Characterized by defiance and arguing, the child will assume "no" as his/her favorite word. He/she will refuse to listen to the teacher, ignoring both rules and requests. The teacher might also notice him/her being vengeful, with all of this behavior causing a struggle in connection to learning.

Such children often have difficulties making friends, as they do not know how to properly interact with their peers. Their schoolwork is often affected and, as a result, there is a significant risk of depression and/or anxiety. These are the children who might develop a conduct disorder later in life, or resort to drug abuse.

The family of the child with ODD should be in constant communication with the teacher and school counselor, as the common goal is to reduce the negative manifestations and improve behavior overall. Children with ODD should be supported in learning about positive interactions with peers. Specialized plans can be developed for behavior management, so the child can improve both socially and academically. Ultimately, the teacher should reinforce what the parents are trying to do at home, showing consistency.

Power struggles should be avoided

Just like parents at home, teachers should pick their battles and not engage in arguments with their students. One should always remember that such children are experts when it comes to getting in an argument. It is up to the teacher to choose the fights worth pursuing. Moreover, one should be correct and acknowledge if a mistake has been made, as this represents a valuable lesson for the child with ODD.

When responding to a defiant child, one should act as if a business transaction is being completed. All responses should be calm and brief, with the teacher avoiding being sarcastic or using negative attributes to describe what has happened. The behavior of the teacher and, most importantly, the way he/she responds can determine whether or not the child will continue to be defiant.

Responses given calmly and neutrally will increase compliance in children with ODD. One should also remember that a short response does not give the child enough time to assume control over the situation.

Moreover, it will prevent the teacher from offering more negative attention to the child, which can only add to the problem behavior.

Consistency above all else

Children who suffer from a behavioral issue need consistency, including in the classroom. One should avoid arguments, as well as repeating the same words or threatening with one consequence after the other. Instead, it is a good idea to use specific words to signify that a situation or action will have consequences. Within the classroom, one can also designate a special place where the child can go when he/she needs to calm down.

Choices allow the child to feel in control

At the beginning of the chapter, we mentioned that children with ODD like to feel in control. This can be easily guaranteed by giving the child the freedom to make certain choices. However, when offering the chance to choose between two things, make sure that he/she has enough time to process the information and make a sound decision.

Breaks matter a lot to a child with ODD

As children grow, they might learn to recognize when they are feeling overwhelmed or on the verge of getting into an argument. Parents might talk to the teacher about creating a safe space, as mentioned above, in which the child can calm down.

Provided with this space, the child might be able to make better choices. This can be especially beneficial after a hard task has been accomplished or after activities that provided a lot of stimulation. Just make sure this is not perceived as a punishment, such as being sent into a corner for everyone to see.

Positive reinforcement for positive results

Positive reinforcement is something all children need. With ODD, it can be the single most effective tool for changing a problematic behavior into one that is adequate. The teacher can offer his/her student(s) the possibility of earning privileges for doing good things.

Often, teachers punish their students who are defiant or oppositional by taking away their privileges. This form of punishment never pays off, as opposed to positive reinforcement. A reward system might also be used for smaller children, but it is the responsibility of the teacher to make sure it is appropriate and not perceived in the wrong manner (such as manipulation).

A personal connection can go a long way

Children with ODD can benefit tremendously from a close relationship with their teacher. Aside from parents, this is one of the people he/she spends the most time with, and a good teacher will be useful in pointing out the best ways for dealing with problematic behavior.

Teachers should refrain from constantly drawing attention to the negative behavior and rather use the time to build a personal connection with the child. It is essential to get to the root of the behavior and work together, to establish behavioral goals. They might also present the child with the consequences to be considered when such goals fail to be met.

Active listening is a skill all teachers should possess. Children need to see that their teacher is genuinely interested in their concerns, even when they are at their lowest point. One should also remember that children with ODD do not know how to negotiate, often becoming angry and defensive in less than a minute. Teachers should listen to their students, trying to respect their point of view and never putting them down just because they are authority figures.

Open-ended questions can help a lot

If a negative situation has occurred, the teacher has a better chance of interacting with the confrontational student by asking open-ended questions. These will help identify triggers associated with the problematic behavior, as well as to gather all the necessary information before responding to the situation.

In asking such questions, one might use "who," "where," "what," "when" and "how." These will help the student detail what happened and also identify the best possible solutions to come to a resolution. Attention: one should avoid asking "why," as this will suggest you have already decided who the guilty party is.

Ask the student to write a reflective essay

Misbehavior is something children with ODD are quite familiar with. Once a negative situation has taken place, the teacher might ask the child in question to write a reflective essay about it. The child should describe why the situation has occurred and what they plan to do to improve their behavior. They might also talk about the role they played, other students involved and problem resolutions. Suggestions might also be provided on how such situations can be prevented in the future.

Do not be afraid to praise the student for something well done

Even though children with ODD are often deemed oppositional and defiant, one should not expect them to be like that all the time. When the student has completed a task as requested, the teacher should offer specific praise, without embarrassing the student.

All students respond well to praise, but keep in mind, children are quite sensitive to honesty. The praise must be sincere and detailed and offered immediately. Teachers should be as descriptive as possible when offering praise. Otherwise, they will not be deemed honest and the child will not be certain whether he/she has matched the expectations of the teacher or not.

Always remember that there are a lot of children who do not like to be praised in front of their peers. If public praise is not something they are comfortable with, one might take another approach. For example, the teacher might write a note praising the child, and give it to him/her in a discreet manner.

It is difficult for children with ODD to go through a normal school day without getting into arguments or fights. Collaboration between parents and teachers is essential to ensure behavioral goals will be faster reached and the child can improve his/her academic performance.

CHAPTER 17 – HOW TO TREAT SPOILED BEHAVIOR

Most parents do not even realize that they are spoiling their child. They simply want the best for them, and are trying to compensate for the things they lacked in their own childhood. However, when the child already suffers from a behavioral issue such as ODD, spoiling him/her will only make matters worse.

How do you recognize a spoiled child?

A spoiled child will not respect his/her parents and other authority figures. Aside from rudeness, he/she might refuse to share toys with other children. He/she will act like the boss in a group, demanding to take part first in various activities. Refusing to answer questions, he/she will ignore the instructions given by adults.

Of course, sometimes it can be difficult to determine which behavior is caused by ODD and which is the result of a child being spoiled. Well, a tantrum is still a tantrum, no matter the reason. And the most important thing is not to feel defeated or helpless. Keep in mind that it all starts with you, the parent, and the way you behave with the child.

Be willing to change and so will your child

As it can take a while for ODD behavior to improve, it might be easier to make the necessary corrections when it comes to spoiling your child. It all begins with you admitting that you have spoiled your child and making a promise to yourself that things are going to change.

Keep in mind that a spoiled child will only turn into a spoiled teenager, who will be self-absorbed and have issues with self-control. If no measures are taken to address the problematic behavior, the teenager is at risk of becoming chronically anxious or depressed.

Parents tend to offer their child everything. The earlier this starts, the harder it will be for the child to be satisfied with his/her life. A spoiled child can get easily frustrated, causing the parents to offer even more things, due to their frustration at the relationship. The solution is to tread on a different path and teach children to be satisfied with less so that they become resilient and capable of handling more difficult times.

Stop spoiling your child, no matter how difficult it might seem

Once you admit to yourself that your child is spoiled, the next obvious step is to stop. You might experience difficulties changing your behavior, but you must commit to this goal, especially if you want your child to be less defiant and oppositional.

Of course, you do not have to go to the extreme and suddenly forbid your child from having anything. What matters is that you gradually reduce unnecessary incentives, teaching your child that it is possible to lead a peaceful existence. As soon as you stop spoiling the child, and after the tantrum-filled period, you will see that his/her behavior has improved.

No child will recognize that he/she is being spoiled. However, you can have a serious discussion about the need to make certain changes. A smart kid will be able to read between the lines. It is far better to have a resilient child than a spoiled one.

No empty threats – clear instructions & consequences

Imagine the following situation. You have asked your child to make his/her bed but he/she keeps playing, ignoring your request. Frustrated, you might say "this is the last time I will ask you," or resort to different strategies, such as counting to three. The longer you are ignored, the easier it will be for you to resort to empty threats.

Children, and especially ones with ODD, do not respond to empty threats. They need to hear exactly what will happen and, most importantly, see you sticking to what has been said. You need to provide them with clear instructions and consequences, as this guarantees the best chance of them listening.

Unfortunately, many parents tend to waste a lot of time explaining themselves to their children. They might also haggle with the child, trying to convince him/her to do a routine task, such as brushing his/her teeth or making the bed. There should be no arguments when it comes to such matters and, as a parent, you should get the last word.

Be consistent where discipline is concerned

Discipline is very important for a child who has been spoiled for a long period. To be successful, you should make sure that your actions speak louder than words. Children do not need endless discussions about behavior improvement, they need to see their parents being consistent with discipline and enforcing consequences.

If your child refuses, for example, to pick up his/her toys or brush his/her teeth, you can mention a specific consequence for each of these two. You can take away his/her screen time or eliminate treats for the day. The child might cry and even have a tantrum, but the most important thing is not to give in.

Keep in mind that you are trying to raise a child who will turn into a resilient adult. Limits are important and you should talk to your child about discipline, its purpose and long-term effect. No child should grow up confusing discipline with lack of love or rejection.

Children do not need to be excessively protected or rescued

Parents need to protect their children and, sometimes, rescue them from difficult situations. But this does not mean you should keep your child in a bubble. As he/she will grow up, the bubble will be too removed from reality and it will be difficult, if not impossible, for the child to become resilient.

It also takes a lot of energy for parents to constantly keep track of the child's needs for protection/rescuing. For instance, if your child does not arrive at school on time, there is no need to threaten them with consequences. You can simply let the child experience the said consequences, as tardiness is punished by the school.

You need to let your child "fall" from time to time, without rushing in to save the day. Even though you are your child's safety net, make sure to be there for him/her only when the situation requires it. Resilience cannot be developed when the child is not allowed to experience certain things on his/her own.

Less material things, more experiences

It is only normal for you, as a parent, to wish for your child to have everything. Sadly, one tends to opt for material things rather than experiences. When children are showered with all sorts of gifts, they learn that everything will be handed to them and it is not necessary to make an effort to earn something by themselves.

In the modern world, children have entire rooms filled with the latest toys, gadgets, and clothes. Parents rarely ask them to save up for a toy, and end up purchasing way more than they need. As a responsible parent, you have to be aware that this is not the right way to raise your child.

If you want your child to be less spoiled, stop overindulging him/her with material things. Instead, ask him/her to save money for a certain toy. Practice gratitude and patience, as these are two of the most important lessons to be learned. Moreover, you will be less stressed about financial matters, as you will cut back on excessive spending.

It is not easy to have a child who suffers from ODD, and who is also spoiled. However, you have to remember that you are the parent and, thus, in control. The spoiled behavior can be easily improved, using the strategies that have been presented above. All it matters is that you are willing to put in the effort.

CHAPTER 18 – MANAGE EXTREME BEHAVIOR

W hen you have a child with ODD, his/her behavior can escalate, to the point that the child becomes aggressive, either verbally or physically. As a parent, it is only normal to ask yourself how you are going to handle aggressive, violent behavior, effectively.

Seeing the bigger picture

A child does not become aggressive or violent without reason. You must be able to see the bigger picture and understand that you are dealing with a child who gets frustrated more easily than his/her peers. More often than not, aggression will be the only solution for them to get out of a conflict. In a way, you can think of this as a "skill" they prefer using.

Not all children reach the point where they become aggressive or violent. But many of them seem always on the edge, causing parents to become frustrated and helpless. You might constantly wonder what will happen if the behavior continues to escalate.

Things are already taken to the extreme, as most kids with ODD resort to telling lies, yelling, disrespecting rules or destroying property. Look at the big picture and try to equip your child with the right skills to handle a conflict-based situation. And, remember, the extreme behavior is not permanent, as long as you fight against it, using the right tools.

Teach your child the right skills for conflict resolution

As adults, we have several skills that we resort to when dealing with unpleasant or difficult situations. These are coping tools or strategies, allowing us to reduce the amount of stress or frustration associated with everyday life. We might call a friend and chat, read a book or practice our favorite sport. Interestingly enough, these skills will change as time passes, and according to individual needs.

When it comes to children and especially those who suffer from oppositional defiant disorder, things are different. They do not have any coping skills, to begin with. And it is the responsibility of the parents to teach them the right skills for dealing with various situations. In deciding how you will help your child cope, take a good look at him/her. Some children need to voice their problems, others might benefit from some alone time, maybe listening to music or reading a book.

It is also true that kids with ODD have difficulties handling emotional challenges. Even when their parents have introduced some coping skills, they might have a hard time selecting and using the right skill. Frustration appears immediately and aggression is the first choice for resolving conflict.

The state of conflict is accompanied and often caused by a rush of adrenaline. Children who suffer from behavioral issues cannot select the most effective coping skills for managing an outburst of energy. They become frustrated and angry when trying to decide how they should proceed. For this reason, it makes sense to them to punch a hole in the wall, cause other damage to property or become aggressive towards peers or adults.

Choose a moment of calm and talk to your child

Parents know their children inside and out. Listen to your instinct and do not contribute to the escalation of a conflict, especially if you feel like the child is on the edge of an outburst.

Choose a moment of calm and talk to your child, explaining to him/her that you are concerned about his/her extreme behavior and the consequences it might have. You can mention that you noticed him/her become angry and that you want to help him/her deal with such situations more effectively.

Let your child know that physical aggression is known as assault, which is punishable by law. Make it clear that you will never accept physical abuse, not even when it comes from him/her. This discussion will help your child understand that actions have consequences, as well as that boundaries must be respected at all times and extreme behavior, especially the ones that involve aggression, will not be tolerated.

If you are dealing with a child who is frequently aggressive, you might resort to calling the police. In this way, your child will learn that such behavior does have a clear consequence and that violence of any kind is never to be accepted. Children with ODD, and especially teenagers, can benefit from such lessons, as they need to understand that there is no excuse for abusing other people.

A plan for the next conflict

Depending on the age of your child, you might consider working together and coming up with a plan for how to handle conflict the next time it arises. Take your time to explain what happens when adrenaline rushes through the body and feelings of anger, frustration or irritation appear.

Come up with solutions he/she can try when feeling on the edge, making sure that you let him/her know it is all right to voice his/her feelings. You might recommend physical exercise, as this can help reduce the amount of adrenaline in the body.

Once again, keep in mind the individuality of your child when developing this plan. While a particular child might benefit from taking a walk through the park, another would gain more by sitting in his/her room and listening to music. Introverted children might prefer drawing or writing in a journal, as these activities will bring a state of calm more quickly.

You might also ask the child whether he/she has any ideas or suggestions on how to deal with an escalating situation, and reduce the extreme behavior. What matters is that the child feels involved, putting his/her mind to good use. You can teach him/her about identifying emotions and the best ways of dealing with them in a manner that does not include aggression or violence.

This cannot be stated enough, but it is important for parents to avoid power struggles, as these are often triggers of both verbal and physical aggression. You are the one in charge of reducing the intensity of a situation before everything gets blown out of proportion.

Raising a child who exhibits extreme behavior can be exhausting and quite frustrating. As parents, however, we already have several effective coping skills that we might use. The one thing not to do is give in to the adrenaline rush ourselves, yelling, arguing or blaming the child. In such situations, we should withdraw and try to model a calm approach. Remember, it is not about winning or towering over the child, but rather about helping him/her improve his/her behavior and overall well-being.

CHAPTER 19 – CREATE HEALTHY LONG–TERM RELATIONSHIPS

T
he aftermath of the behavioral issue might be so severe that it permanently damages the relationship between the parent and the child. Many children who suffer from ODD will develop a conduct disorder later on in life, which will damage the parent-child relationship even further. This is, however, only one way for things can go.

If parents work not only on improving the behavior of the child, but also the relationship between them, chances are they will be just as close in adulthood. It might mean making a little more effort to cement the connection and always remembering that he/she is your child, needing to be loved above all else.

Spend time with your child

Children need one-on-one time with their parents, as this is highly important for their development, especially when it comes to self-awareness and self-esteem. You do not have to do anything complicated; what matters is that you talk to your child and show interest in what he/she has to say.

When you spend time with your child, he/she will feel appreciated and know that you are always there. A child with ODD might have difficulties expressing or even identifying how he/she feels, so be patient. You need to provide ample opportunities for self-expression, helping the child become more confident in his/her coping skills and never forgetting that love is the most important thing to give a child.

During these moments, you can model to your child how emotions and feelings should be expressed healthily. He/she will learn that he/she can put his/her trust in you, as well as that he/she should always feel safe to come to you. A good parent will respect his/her child, validating his/her feelings and opinions, and correcting misbehavior when necessary.

Spending time with the child matters more than you might think. Even when you are just sitting together and talking, you are helping your child accumulate valuable skills for later on in life. He/she is learning how to express his/her emotions healthily, and how to handle adult life, without seeking validation from others.

Hug your child for a stronger connection

You might not expect hugging to count as such an important thing but, as research confirms, children need at least four hugs per day to survive. Eight hugs are necessary for maintenance, while twelve hugs ensure that children will grow into healthy adults.

Just because you have a child who is dealing with behavioral issues, this does not mean you should not hug him/her every chance you get. Try to develop a morning routine that includes at least several minutes of snuggling, and do the same before going to bed. Give him/her a hug when he/she goes to school and one when he/she comes back. Offer many more hugs throughout the day.

A hug is not the only way to establish a physical connection with your child. You can pat him/her on the back, play with his/her hair or give him/her a kiss. Always maintain eye contact and smile, as children need these gestures of reassurance. Keep in mind that you are creating the foundation for the future, and do not forget that your child – even as an adult – will benefit from a close relationship.

Play with your child

You might think you are too old for playing, but in reality, this experience is beneficial for adults and children alike. When you turn into a child again, engaging in various activities and laughing your heart out, you create a positive atmosphere. Happiness hormones are released in the brain, and the child will most likely forget about feeling angry or frustrated. Make play a daily goal and do your best to put a smile on your child's face.

If you refuse to play with your child, you might have a hard time forming a connection with him/her. On the other hand, by playing, you can create memories that he/she will cherish for the rest of his/her life. Play can replace anger easily, allowing the child to no longer feel disconnected, reducing the opportunities for him/her to act out. Moreover, structured play increases cooperation, focus, and attention to detail.

Dedicate your attention exclusively to the child

We live in the era of smartphones, where everyone seems to be more attached to their devices than their own family. When interacting with your child, do your best to stop browsing social media and pay attention to him/her. A child who feels ignored might resort to undesirable ways to get you attentive, becoming physically aggressive, yelling or destroying things.

Children need exclusive attention. And they will remember how their parents stopped everything they were doing and listened to them. So, put down your phone, stop listening to music or watching that movie. Connect with your child, looking him/her in the eye and making sure he/she knows he/she is being heard. In this way, the child will find it easier to open up and discuss his/her misbehavior.

Do not ask your child to refrain from expressing his/her emotions

People become parents without necessarily recovering from their own childhood. They might have been taught that it is not all right for them to express emotions, and thus, they might be tempted to ask the same from their children. Nonetheless, it is quite damaging to expect any child to hide how he/she feels, let alone a child who suffers from ODD.

It might be inconvenient for you in the beginning, but you have to remember that expressing emotions is a healthy thing. It will help both you and your child understand the associated behavioral issues, and, as part of the big picture, it will bring the two of you closer together.

Your child needs empathy first and foremost. If he/she feels like crying, let him/her cry. What matters is that you offer him/her a safe place, in which he/she can express his/her feelings, even if it means letting out some tears. Acknowledge his/her suffering and move through the emotions experienced, so that he/she can get back to his/her routine.

When parents take the time to process emotions together with the child, the connection between them becomes stronger than ever. Children dwell in the safety offered by their parents and, even if ODD is an issue, you will see that the child is more relaxed and cooperative after such moments. As a parent, you might also want to work on regulating your emotions, so that your childhood wounds do not create fresh ones within your child.

We cannot foretell the future. But we can do our best to ensure that our child's behavior improves and he/she will turn into a healthy adult. To create a healthy, long-term relationship with your child, you need to be there for him/her when he/she needs you the most.

Provide your child with a safe space to express his/her emotions, listen to any concerns he/she might have and do not hesitate to slow down, enjoying every moment spent together. Children need to know that their parents are there for them, so make sure you are the kind of parent your child needs.

CHAPTER 20 – HOW TO START NOW

N ow that you have familiarized yourself with oppositional defiant disorder, it is time to make a plan for action. We are going to walk you through the steps this plan might include, summarizing everything you need to remember.

1. Start looking for red flags

You have probably suspected for some time that your child is not just defiant but that there is an actual problem. If your child seems angry, easily irritable or prone to breaking rules, he/she might suffer from ODD.

2. Is it a developmental problem or a learned behavior?

Time to visit a specialist. Using several assessment tools and direct observation, the psychologist/psychiatrist will decide whether your child suffers from ODD or not and if he/she has an associated developmental issue. He/she will consider other potential conditions, such as conduct disorder, antisocial personality or ADHD. Diagnosis is usually made after the age of four.

3. Look at the potential factors leading to ODD

Genetics matter quite a lot, as behavioral issues tend to be present in several members of the same family. The same goes for developmental issues and inconsistent parenting practices, especially those that are based on negative interactions.

4. Parenting style – what kind of behavior does the child learn from you?

Perhaps this is the most difficult thing to acknowledge – you playing a part in the behavioral issue. However, parenting style does influence the appearance of ODD, even though it is not the only causative factor. You have to model the right behavior to your child, avoiding negative reinforcement.

5. Mental health issues – making ODD worse

Both children and teenagers can suffer from mental health issues, which can make the manifestations of ODD worse. Discuss with the specialist about such matters, as this behavioral issue is often diagnosed in children/teenagers who also suffer from anxiety, depression or learning disabilities.

6. Early intervention for better prognosis

Once the diagnosis of ODD has been made, it is time to seek out solutions. The earlier therapy is started, the better the long-term prognosis is going to be. It is for the best to find someone who specializes in correcting the defiant and oppositional behavior.

7. Remember that each child is different

Even though all children/teenagers with ODD will present similar manifestations, parents should remember that each child is different. Just because something has worked with another child, it does not mean your child will respond in the same way.

8. Model the behavior you wish to see from the child

Children consider parents to be their role models, unconsciously imitating everything they do. If you want your child's behavior to improve, you have to be the best role model you can be. Avoid power struggles, as these will only make matters worse. You want your child's behavior to improve and this should never be about winning.

9. Decisions & choices

Children are less likely to engage in defiant or oppositional behavior when they are involved in the decision-making process or when parents give them choices. However, there should also be non-negotiable rules that they must respect, with well-chosen consequences they will suffer from if they do not obey.

10. Routine & consistency

All children benefit from a well-established routine and this is even more important for a child who struggles to adopt the correct behavior. Be consistent in everything you do and you will see your child doing the same.

11. Spend time together

Often, oppositional or defiant behavior appears as the child feels neglected by his/her parents. Do your best to spend quality time together, dedicating your complete attention to your child. Remember, however, that you are his/her parent and not a friend, so there will be some moments when rules must be enforced.

12. Address the wrong behavior right away

If your child behaves inadequately, you should address the behavior in question right away. Using a calm approach, talk about the consequences that will be enforced. Resort to discipline rather than punishment, as the latter rarely gives the results you'd expect.

13. Communicate with your child in a healthy manner

Children who suffer from a behavioral issue such as ODD need to communicate with their parents, but rarely know how to do that. As the parent, ensure healthy communication by using a calm tone, choosing specific code words for calming down and resorting to positive language. Do not forget to make eye contact, as this will further facilitate communication.

14. Teach your child how to create healthy boundaries

You are the best person in the world to teach your child about healthy boundaries. Start by defining these and the expectations you have, teaching your child about self-respect and crossing boundaries. Impose consequences, but show yourself to be understanding in less severe situations. Avoid placing labels and talk about limits instead.

15. Overcome obstacles together

When raising a child with ODD, you might come across many obstacles. Partner up with your child and do your best to overcome these obstacles together. Pay attention to your behavior and learn how to ask something from him/her. Try looking at things from his/her perspective and do not be afraid to change the context for the desired behavior.

16. Respect your child

Your child is more than his/her current behavior. And he/she needs respect. Try to see beyond the ODD, and act as a responsible and loving parent. Offer your child structure and do not forget about empathy. Avoid belittling him/her and rather, spend your time identifying and expressing emotions together.

17. What happens at school?

Parents and teachers should work together to handle a child who suffers from ODD. Teachers, like parents, should avoid power struggles and be consistent when it comes to their behavior. Children should be given choices, as well as breaks and safe spaces to recollect and calm down. Positive reinforcement is more than helpful, as well as establishing a personal connection with the child.

18. Address spoiled behavior

If you have spoiled your child, you have only made things worse. You need to change your approach. Stop making empty threats and enforce useful consequences. Be consistent in your discipline and offer your child more experiences, as opposed to material things.

19. Handle any extreme behavior in the right manner

Extreme behavior is something all children with ODD may experience and it is up to the parents to handle such situations, without causing any further damage. Children should be taught the right skills for conflict resolution and a plan should be made for how conflicts should be resolved in the future. Think like this: You are equipping your child with the right tools (emotions) to handle demanding situations in a healthy manner.

20. Work for a healthy, long-term relationship

You can lay the foundation for a healthy, long-term relationship by spending more time with your child. You can play together, hug and kiss, or watch his/her favorite cartoons. What matters is that you express emotions together, creating memories to be cherished for many years to come.

Sometimes, it might be a good idea to cast everything aside and just love your child. Remember that he/she becomes easily frustrated and irritated, looking at the world as if it were filled only with negative things. You are his/her safe space and love can heal many wounds, helping your child improve his/her behavior.

CASE STUDIES

Casey, 40 years, adult-age diagnosis of ODD

Casey is a woman in her 40s, who has just found out that she might be suffering from an oppositional defiant disorder that has transferred well into adulthood. Her mother declared that Casey began to exhibit oppositional and defiant behavior around the age of four. She constantly tried to get attention from her mother by moving things around the house.

The behavior disturbed the mother, as she liked to have an organized household. When she reprimanded Casey for her behavior, things only got worse. Perhaps it would have been a lot better if the mother had taken part in her games, rather than constantly admonishing her behavior. Casey unconsciously learned that this is the way to respond to most situations.

Later on, Casey's parents separated and she had to live with her father, the relationship with her mother remaining unresolved. She relied on oppositional and defiant behavior to cope with all the changes, experiencing difficulties at school as well as making only a few friends.

During college, she constantly complained that her teachers were unfair, and had a hard time meeting academic demands. In her personal life, she was unable to maintain a relationship for more than several months. She changed studies several times, once again blaming other people for her failure.

Casey was wrongfully diagnosed with depression, even though she did not even manifest symptoms characteristic of this condition. When talking to one of her best friends about the diagnosis, and once again complaining about how everything goes wrong, the subject of ODD came up.

Her friend had come across an article online, highlighting all of the manifestations associated with the condition. She immediately recognized these in Casey and printed the article. When Casey saw everything that was written, it did not take more than a minute to recognize the issues to be resolved – in a short time, her life improved and she managed to commit to a new partner.

It took Casey such a long time to understand what was happening. The good thing is that this is a behavioral issue, which is easy to recognize and control through clear measures. Casey resorted to therapy, to become less oppositional and defiant, letting go of all the anger and frustration. She now lives a full, normal life.

Matthew, 14 years old, diagnosed with ODD at 12

Matthew used to come home from school and complain that he was being bullied. He also said that his teachers constantly undermined him. His parents reported that he had changed schools several times, after being diagnosed with a mild form of autism. His grades were average and there was no indication of behavioral issues, at least not in the school records.

A psychologist came to observe him in the school setting. He saw that Matthew preferred to spend a lot of his time drawing, rather than completing the tasks he was asked. Moreover, he blamed the other kids for him not having done the work as requested.

In one of the first therapy sessions, the psychologist asked Matthew if he liked school. Without making eye contact, he responded "no." When referring to the drawing, however, the boy not only looked the therapist right in the eye, but he started talking with passion.

Upon spending more time at school, observing Matthew, the psychologist noted that he had become accustomed to blaming others for his mistakes. The behavior was not acknowledged by teachers. A meeting with the family was organized and it was clear that the father was the authority figure. He gave the children commands to obey, and they were not allowed to speak freely. Moreover, the mother presented signs of abuse (bruises on the hand).

The father complained of Matthew's behavior, wanting to send him to a military school. The psychologist convinced the father to wait several months before making a final decision, during which the boy would come in for regular therapy sessions.

With ODD, there is always a bigger picture to look at. For Matthew, the picture included abuse, neglect, violence, and instability. The boy believed that he was the guilty party, resorting to coping skills that were anything but beneficial. He had become accustomed to lying, defying authority and showing opposition. The only thing he cared about was drawing.

In therapy, the psychologist became close to Matthew by talking about his passion – drawing. They discussed technique, themes, and even architecture, with the boy becoming communicative and bonding with the therapist. With time, he came out of his shell and started talking about his feelings.

Therapy helped Matthew improve his behavior, not only at home, but also in the school setting. He was advised to keep a journal, in which he could express his feelings and, most importantly, any concerns he might have. After the parents divorced, Matthew went to live with his grandparents. His academic performance improved significantly. He still goes to therapy.

Leah, 5 years old, diagnosed with ODD at 4

Leah developed oppositional defiant disorder when her father started to work abroad. It was only through therapy that her behavior improved. The therapist also suggested that she would benefit from structured play, in which she could take control. The play sessions, in which the mother would do as the daughter pleased, would also allow her to express how she felt.

This was a clear case in which the oppositional and defiant behavior appeared due to the little girl feeling like she had lost her father. She had difficulty expressing how she felt, given her young age. Her behavior appeared as she struggled to adjust to living only with her mother, feeling the need to be in control all of the time.

It all began with Leah wetting the bed at night, despite having been potty trained for some time. Soon after, the girl started to refuse to comply with her mother's demands. She became defiant and oppositional, with temper tantrums taking place both at home and outside. The behavior occurred after the father left for his new job, in another country.

Leah constantly argued with her mother, throwing her toys and even becoming aggressive. The mother took her to a specialist, who excluded organic causes for the bed-wetting. There was no reason to consider that Leah suffered from a mood disorder or a developmental delay. It was then that the therapist talked about the parent-child attachment deficit and how it could lead to ODD.

Therapy was started as soon as the diagnosis had been made. Even though the therapist asked Leah how she felt about her father leaving, she was unable to answer. However, during play therapy, she made up games in which she would talk about being sad. It was through play that she decided to express how she felt.

At the recommendation of the therapist, the mother started to use time-outs as consequences for misbehavior. This led to fewer temper tantrums, especially outside the house. Nonetheless, Leah continued to be oppositional and defiant, trying to control her immediate environment.

The structured play sessions that took place at home led to the desired breakthrough. She was allowed to choose the games and be in complete control, which in turn offered her plenty of opportunities to express her feelings. Soon, she gave up the need to be in control.

Leah still goes to therapy but the results are noticeable. The therapist has recommended that the girl is kept in regular contact with her father, as this is more than beneficial. One year into therapy, Leah is less oppositional and no longer tries to dominate her mother. She is more compliant, both at home and in other settings, such as kindergarten.

Gabriel, 16 years old, diagnosed with ODD at 7

At the age of seven, it was clear that something was not right. Gabriel's parents were worried about his attitude towards school and authority in general. He refused to complete assignments, his teacher complaining of him being defiant and oppositional.

At home, Gabriel would lose his temper easily, being furious and frustrated all of the time. He screamed at his parents and used offensive language. In class, he would have frequent violent outbursts, which led to him being avoided by his peers.

In light of all these behaviors, his parents decided to take him to a specialist. The therapist identified a pattern of behavior, presenting the parents with oppositional defiant disorder as a potential diagnosis. After all, Gabriel lost his temper, preferred arguing and defying authority, being angry and vindictive.

Talking to the parents, the specialist discovered that there was a lot of fighting going on between them. Moreover, there was a family history of behavioral issues. Gabriel, it seemed, had all the prerequisites for ODD. Therapy was started and the parents decided to go to counseling as well.

Unfortunately, parental marital discord continued, which prevented Gabriel from improving a lot. As a teenager, he still struggles with ODD, which continues to affect his academic performance and social life. Learning disabilities and ADHD have been excluded as co-existent conditions.

Gabriel continued to go to therapy, struggling to separate himself from what happens at home. The therapist recommended the parents closely monitor the teen, as there is a high risk of drug abuse. Parent management training helped both his mom and dad understand that, even as a teenager, Gabriel needs a peaceful home environment.

The decision for the parents to separate was welcomed by Gabriel. He lives now with his mother and the behavior has improved significantly. He is less frustrated and angry, which in turn is beneficial for the mom. She tries to ensure a structured routine, being empathetic towards his needs as a teenager. The dad also spends time with Gabriel.

CONCLUSION

P arents want the best for their children. When faced with a behavioral issue, it is easy to forget that the respective child still needs to be loved. Throughout this book, we have emphasized that, just because your child suffers from ODD, this does not mean you should not show him/her love, respect, and validation.

We hope that, by now, you have gained an in-depth understanding of oppositional defiant disorder. You have probably concluded why your child suffers from ODD and acknowledged the fact that this condition can co-exist with other issues, such as ADHD, anxiety or depression.

You can look at this book as your guide to surviving life with a child who is both oppositional and defiant. And, most importantly, it will help you understand that this diagnosis is only the beginning of a long but rewarding fight. You now have all the tools to change your parenting for the better and consolidate the relationship with your child, supporting him/her in improving his/her behavior.

Perhaps the most important lesson to take from this book is that ODD rarely goes away on its own. Almost all children or teenagers who suffer from behavioral issues need therapy, and some might even require medication. Therapy must be continued even after improvements have been noticed and parents should be actively involved in the process.

For parents, dealing with a child who throws temper tantrums can be frustrating, to say the least. You have probably felt helpless countless of times, wondering how you should handle a particular situation. Hopefully we have provided you with numerous solutions for dealing with such a child, reducing the tantrums, as well as the opposition and defiance. Remember, however, that things will not change overnight and you have to be perseverant. Your child needs you to be strong and consistent, and, most importantly, to know that you are on his/her side.

Never assume that your child does not have anything to say. Be an active listener and you might help the child come out of his/her shell, voicing any concerns he/she might have. You might be surprised to discover that children are often worried about their behavior, considering themselves to be at fault for everything that happens.

Talk to your child and give him/her time to respond. Discuss consequences associated with misbehavior and design a plan for action. Involve the child in the decision-making process, when appropriate, and offer him/her choices. Do not be afraid to impose limits and help your child understand what healthy boundaries are all about.

With teenagers, things might be just as difficult. They often feel misunderstood, avoiding interaction with their parents – the last thing they want is to be judged. Parenting a teen with ODD can be hell, but it can also be an opportunity for you to change the relationship for the better. Go to therapy together and find out what upsets him/her. Be there for your child and he/she will stay on the right track.

We hope that, in dealing with your oppositional and defiant child, you will remember that connection should always come before correction. Do not give in to your own childhood trauma and remember that your child may feel hurt, rejected or simply sad. Connect first, so that the child feels safe enough to provide details on how he/she feels. You can then discuss correcting his/her behavior.

Both children and teenagers with ODD struggle at school; they constantly defy authority, get into fights with peers and seek revenge. We have talked about the best solutions for improving behavior at school – the most important thing is that parents collaborate with teachers, to address the behavioral issues from more than one angle.

We have mentioned that the child should be loved above all else. However, this does not mean that you should spoil him/her excessively, as this will only aggravate the problematic behavior. Do not be afraid to impose limits and consequences, acting as a parent and not as a friend. Even though this might seem to make matters worse initially, the behavior will improve as time passes. You need to stand your ground and help your child learn what respect is all about. Love is just a different thing and it has nothing to do with spoiling the child.

Of course, there will be a lot of times when things will seem blown out of proportion. The child will scream and defy you blatantly, refusing to comply with your demands or throwing temper tantrums in public. The teenager will shut the door in your face, skip school or actively defy teachers. We hope you will use our recommendations for managing such extreme behavior, also resorting to therapy to get the child/teen back on track.

The case studies have been chosen to highlight the experiences of parents raising children or teenagers with ODD and the solutions they used. Read them thoroughly and even several times, as they can offer important information on how the condition was identified, what caused it and how it was addressed. See how it affected the family dynamic and compare these case studies with your own situation.

We hope you have had a great read and that you have found this book to be useful. If you suspect your child or teenager might suffer from oppositional defiant disorder, do not hesitate to visit a specialist and get an accurate diagnosis. Remember, the sooner the intervention is started, the better the outcome is going to be, in the long run. Good luck!

Made in the USA
Monee, IL
17 September 2021

78254918R00066